RIDING WITH THE DOLPHINS

THE EQUINOX GUIDE TO DOLPHINS AND PORPOISES

ERICH HOYT
WITH ILLUSTRATIONS BY PIETER FOLKENS

CAMDEN HOUSE

CAMDEN
•HOUSE•
♦♦♦♦♦
PUBLISHING

Canadian Cataloguing in Publication Data

Hoyt, Erich, 1950-
   Riding with the dolphins : the Equinox
guide to dolphins and porpoises

Includes index.
ISBN 0-921820-55-0 (bound)   ISBN 0-921820-57-7 (pbk.)

1. Dolphins – Juvenile literature.   2. Porpoises –
Juvenile literature.   3. Dolphins.   4. Porpoises.
I. Title.

QL737.C43H69   1992   j599.5'3   C92-094741-7

Front cover photograph by
Scott Sinclair/Earthviews

Back cover photograph by
Norbert Wu

Colour separations by
Hadwen Graphics
Ottawa, Ontario

Printed and bound in Canada by
Tri-Graphic Printing
Ottawa, Ontario

Printed on acid-free paper

Published by Camden House Publishing
(a division of Telemedia Publishing Inc.)

Camden House Publishing
7 Queen Victoria Road
Camden East, Ontario K0K 1J0

Camden House Publishing
Box 766
Buffalo, New York 14240-0766

Trade distribution by
Firefly Books
250 Sparks Avenue
Willowdale, Ontario
Canada M2H 2S4

Box 1325
Ellicott Station
Buffalo, New York 14205

CONTENTS

INTRODUCTION

It was the most peaceful scene imaginable. As the sun broke through the morning fog, several related families of orcas, or killer whales—mothers, fathers, youngsters, cousins and grandparents—slipped through a calm, liquid ocean, water trailing off their fins.

For weeks, a group of researchers, I among them, had spent long days travelling with three family groups, or pods, of orcas living off Canada's northern Vancouver Island. While we grew to know them as individuals and as families, we had enjoyed watching them at rest and at play, following them on their travels. We had even given them names—Top Notch, Nicola, Sharky and Stubbs—to match their distinctive dorsal fins. Now, however, a moment of truth had arrived.

On the distant horizon, we spotted some strange spouts. At first, we thought they were simply more orcas coming to join the group, but the spouts and dorsal fins of the new arrivals were smaller. As we approached in a small outboard motorboat, we cleaned the fresh spray off our binoculars and determined that two minke whales and half a dozen Dall's porpoises were swimming right into the midst of the orcas.

"Here comes a meal," someone shouted. All of us had read accounts of orcas feeding on the up-to-10-metre-long minke whales and 2-metre-long Dall's porpoises. Scientists had described in detail orcas hunting in packs like wolves, stripping the

skin off the whales and ripping out their tongues. Orcas would stun the porpoises with a flick of the tail and devour them one by one.

We expected a bloody encounter. For two hours, we waited, our small craft bobbing in the sea. Nothing happened. Instead, the three species—minke whales, Dall's porpoises and the 34 orcas we had originally sighted—peacefully combed the tide rips side by side, feeding on schools of fish. We soon realized that the orcas we had been following were confirmed fish-eaters.

It was an important lesson in a summer which taught us over and over again that things are rarely as they seem at first. The real story is always worth digging for and is often far more interesting than what was assumed to be true. This is the case with all science and especially field biology. One new fact in the complex natural world leads to another and another. As the layers peel away, the world is gradually revealed.

But what were we to make of the killer whales of legend? What about the stories we had heard? One day, a

wild, fierce pod of orcas appeared that did not look or behave like the orcas with which we were so familiar. Our resident pods ignored these transient orcas, as we referred to them. Silently and erratically, the interlopers swam through our study area, stalking seals and porpoises. In time, we were able to witness a successful feeding attack by transient orcas. Usually, researchers must spend many hours of observation to see such an event. Over the years, by examining the stomach contents of transients that have died, scientists have confirmed their preferred diet: marine mammals.

The science of studying wild dolphin and porpoise societies—using photography to identify individual animals—is only about two decades old. It is still young enough that cherished assumptions are overturned regularly. That is part of the excitement.

Some of the things that first attracted people to dolphins—their large brains, the possibility of communicating with them, their apparently "peaceful" societies, their friendliness toward humans in the wild and in captivity—are no longer considered to be as accurate or as relevant as was once believed. But there are lots of reasons to be curious about dolphins and porpoises.

On the following pages, we will look at the many different species of dolphins and porpoises—all of those known to live in the northern hemisphere, including the river dolphins

An orca, or killer whale, *far left*, slips through the calm waters off northern Vancouver Island, British Columbia. This approachable species has been studied intensively since the early 1970s. Although called killer whale, it is actually the largest dolphin, growing up to 9.8 metres long and weighing as much as 5,000 kilograms. As part of an aquarium show, a young bottlenose dolphin, *left*, at Sea Life Park in Hawaii, leaps high into the air for a fish reward. The orca and the bottlenose dolphin are the most popular and well-known dolphins. Both species live in every ocean, in inshore as well as offshore waters, and have been frequently kept in aquariums and marine parks. These adaptable animals are capable of a wide range of behaviours. Not simply ''warriors of the sea'' that eat anything and everything, orcas are at times crafty, opportunistic predators which use highly developed social skills to catch their food. Likewise, bottlenose dolphins, although showing an overriding curiosity about everything in their world, can occasionally be aggressive.

found in the Tropics. Each species has its own peculiarities and strategies for survival. Each has particular food preferences and feeding behaviours as well as a different habitat – its own niche, or place, in the water.

While most whales range throughout the world ocean, many dolphins and porpoises are limited to one hemisphere, one part of an ocean or, in the case of river dolphins, one river system. Mainly because of their limited ranges, several species of dolphins and porpoises are more endangered than are the large whales, such as the blue, humpback and gray. (These whales were introduced in an earlier companion book, *Meeting the Whales*, but will sometimes be referred to here, since many features of evolution and biology are the same for all whales, dolphins and porpoises.)

We will learn about the dolphins' hearing abilities, their mating and reproductive habits and the fishing-net and pollution problems that threaten their survival. We will discover the fastest swimmers and the best bowriders. We will witness examples of clever feeding behaviour – bottlenose dolphins chasing fish onto a beach, then charging clear out of the water and grabbing the fish before rolling back into the surf. We will spend time with various species in their close, long-term family groups. We will discuss experiments scientists have conducted in an effort to teach bottlenose dolphins a symbolic language.

As we find out more and more about the sea and its residents, we

begin to recognize the vital importance of habitat. In the final chapter, we will examine this often-neglected dimension of research and management programmes. This book will also explore a new way of looking at these fascinating creatures and will present the results of the latest research. Good science is needed to determine the habitat requirements of dolphins and porpoises species by species – an expensive, time-consuming task. Once it is done, humans will be better able to reserve a secure home for dolphins and porpoises, one that will allow these captivating mammals to survive into the next century and beyond.

Spinner dolphins, found only in warm temperate to tropical waters, are renowned for their high, spinning leaps. These spinners, *left*, were photographed in Hawaii, where they have been studied both in captivity and in the wild. The bottlenose dolphin, *above*, investigates coral reefs off the Bahamas, a common living—and hiding—spot for many fish species. The inquisitive nature of the bottlenose dolphin and its use of different feeding techniques has led it to colonize habitats all over the world.

IS IT A DOLPHIN, A PORPOISE—OR A WHALE?

Some of the main differences between a dolphin and a porpoise can be noted by comparing their body shapes. The dolphin, represented by a striped dolphin (top), has a long, relatively slender body and a pronounced beak. The porpoise (bottom), in this case a Dall's porpoise, is generally chunkier and not as big, with a smaller head and no beak. When porpoises or dolphins strand on a beach, scientists are able to tell them apart by examining their teeth. At sea, their social groupings and behaviours also provide strong clues. Dolphins typically travel in much larger groups and are far more likely to go bow-riding. The six species of true porpoises live mainly close to shore, but many dolphins are real world citizens and can be found in several climatic regions in every part of the vast world ocean.

What are the differences between a dolphin, a porpoise and a whale? As it turns out, what appears to be a simple question is not easily answered. Certain dolphins are called whales, including the largest dolphin – the killer whale, or orca. Some fishermen tend to use the word porpoise for all dolphins and porpoises, while others use the word dolphin for both. To confuse matters further, there happens to be a white saltwater fish that is referred to as dolphin; it is a popular restaurant fish that tastes like snapper or cod. Also called mahi-mahi, the dolphinfish has nothing to do with the air-breathing mammals we know as dolphins and porpoises.

True dolphins and porpoises, as well as whales, belong to the order of mammals known as Cetacea, which comes from the Greek word for sea monster. Cetaceans are either baleen or toothed whales, a division that is based primarily on feeding habits.

Baleen whales strain huge mouthfuls of small fish, shrimplike crustaceans and other tiny prey from the water. The strainers are plates that grow from the roof of the mouth. The large whales, such as the blue and the bowhead, are baleen whales.

Toothed whales hunt individual prey and swallow it whole. Dolphins and porpoises are all toothed whales. With the exception of the sperm whale and certain beaked whales, toothed whales are smaller in size than baleen whales.

There are only six porpoise species, sometimes called "true porpoises,"

four of which live in the northern hemisphere. Porpoises are smaller in size than whales and dolphins and have a low dorsal fin (one species has no dorsal fin at all) and, most distinctively, no beak. Most are shy, live close to shore and are less likely to ride alongside the bows of ships than are dolphins.

The two main groups of dolphins are the river dolphin, a group that includes 4 species in the northern hemisphere, and the oceanic dolphin, with 22 species. The oceanic dolphin is the largest family of toothed whales and contains most of the species presented in this book. The basic difference between the two is that the river dolphin lives in rivers and the oceanic dolphin lives mostly in the open ocean, but there are some exceptions.

There are other important differences as well. Compared with the oceanic dolphin, the river dolphin generally has smaller teeth and more of them, a longer beak and poorer vision. The oceanic dolphin is the creature most of us picture when we hear the word dolphin. The bottlenose and common dolphins are two of the best-known oceanic species. Also included, however, are six dolphin species that have the word whale in their names: melon-headed whale, pygmy killer whale, false killer whale, killer whale, long-finned pilot whale and short-finned pilot whale. Indeed, all of these species are toothed whales – as are all other dolphins and porpoises – but they are also members of the family of oceanic dolphins.

Dolphins and porpoises have evolved along similar paths and have much in common with each other and with whales. All have a streamlined shape. All have powerful tails, or flukes, which they move up and down to propel themselves through the water. All have a pair of flippers – modified forelimbs with four or five "finger" bones – that assist with steering. And most species, but not all, have a dorsal fin.

The source of much curiosity, the dorsal fin is sometimes all we see of the dolphin in the wild. What is it used for? Why does a species such as the orca have a dorsal fin up to 180 centimetres tall, while the dorsal fin of other species measures only 20 centimetres?

The dolphin dorsal fin contains no bones; it is made of fibrous cartilage or fatty material. A number of scientists believe its function is similar to that of the keel on a boat, providing stability for the dolphin. With some dolphins, the mature male's dorsal fin is larger than the female's – dramatically so with orcas. A tall dorsal fin may allow males to be easily identified and help females select males for mating. But nothing explains why some dolphins and porpoises, such as the right whale dolphin and the finless porpoise, have no dorsal fin at all. Dorsal fins may serve several purposes, but for certain species, they are obviously not needed.

All dolphins and porpoises have teeth, but the number, shape and size vary considerably with each species. As with other animals, the teeth can sometimes be used to identify the species when carcasses or skulls are discovered.

Most dolphins and porpoises have good vision, and a few can see in colour. In murky river waters, however, vision is of little use, and probably for that reason, some river dolphins have poor or virtually no eyesight. The baiji's eyes are tiny pinholes that let in just enough light to enable it to distinguish shadows.

Rather than external ears, dolphins and porpoises have a tiny opening on both sides of the head that leads to the hearing organs. Yet underwater, dolphins receive sounds through the lower jaw, which channels them to the brain.

Dolphins and porpoises rely on their senses of sight and hearing for hunting. They are also able to taste and can discern certain chemicals in the water. As well, they have an acute sense of touch, reacting even to something as delicate as the stroke of a feather. Their skin is so thin that a sharp fingernail could draw blood, although wounds heal quickly.

The Pacific white-sided dolphin, *left*, reveals the array of sharp, well-separated teeth found in the upper and lower jaws of most dolphins. Notice the pronounced beak, or rostrum. The separation in colours from the dark dorsal, or top, side to the light ventral, or bottom, side is a feature that makes the dolphin less visible to its fish prey. The dark eye, behind and a little above the jawline, is difficult to see except at very close range. The leaping spotted dolphin, *above*, displays the typical streamlined dolphin shape. Its curved-back flippers and dorsal fin provide some stability without reducing the dolphin's speed. Its tail is the power source: the up-and-down movement propels the dolphin through the water, helping it to reach the high speeds that enable it to leap above the surface.

The sense of kinship between humans and dolphins goes back thousands of years. Citizens of ancient Crete honoured dolphins as gods, while the Greeks kept a special sanctuary for what they considered to be the dolphin god. The Maori of the South Pacific regarded dolphins as messengers of the gods. These and other early cultures celebrated the divine features they saw in dolphins.

Dolphins are no longer elevated to the status of gods, but to many people, they are the "humans of the sea" – wise, shrewd and superintelligent. Some aquariums and marine parks contribute to this view by promoting their dolphins as "personalities." Movies, television and science fiction novels do the same thing. To feed our appetite for this connection, stories about breakthroughs in dolphin communication have often been exaggerated by the media.

To be fair, more than one scientist has reported as communication a dolphin's mimicking of an English phrase – something a parrot can do. But despite continuing efforts, researchers have been unable to have conversations with dolphins or to determine whether they do, indeed, have their own spoken language. Although some interspecies communication does exist, it is more akin to what occurs between you and the family dog than to the exchanges you would have with your friends.

Are dolphins superintelligent? The brains of dolphins and porpoises vary in size from one species to another,

but all are fairly large. Yet brain size reveals little about the nature or extent of intelligence. What do dolphins use their brains for? Some researchers have suggested that big brains may be needed for sonar and sound processing or for the demands of social living. But these explanations have been called into question. Others have argued that a dolphin's level of intelligence is somewhere between that of a dog and that of a chimpanzee. The answer is, we don't know, and it may be unfair to make comparisons. Just as human intelligence suits

human needs, dolphin intelligence is perfect for the dolphin's way of life. Until we know more, we can say only that it is different.

What, then, do we know about dolphins? Dolphin research, which is just a few decades old, has caused much excitement. Some behaviour studies have helped verify certain ancient accounts. Although Aristotle recorded that fishermen in the eastern Mediterranean Sea could identify dolphins by the nicks in their fins, generations of humans, including scientists, dismissed it as fable. But Aristotle, who was the first to recognize that dolphins are air-breathing mammals and not fish, seems to have known what he was talking about.

The same is true of 19th-century Australian whalers. At Twofold Bay, whalers came to know individual orcas by name. Hunting in packs, the orcas would help the whalers by chasing a humpback whale, then grabbing its flippers while the whalers made the kill. As the big humpback was towed to shore, the orcas, fond of eating large whales, took only the lips and tongue, leaving the rest of the carcass for the whalers to render for oil. This close and mutually beneficial association between humans and orcas lasted for several decades, until the 1920s.

Today, research into life among wild dolphins reveals that they are curious and apparently sociable. They sometimes even allow people to touch them and swim with them. Ancient Roman stories about boys riding

According to mythology, Pluto, *far left top*, blows his horn to make music to pacify the dolphin he is riding. Note the scaly skin of the big-eyed creature in this early reproduction from a copper engraving—it resembles a dolphin only superficially. Real dolphins, like these bottlenose dolphins, *far left bottom*, are social mammals, fascinating in their own right. The shape of the dolphin's dorsal fin and the marks on its trailing edge help scientists to identify individuals, name them and follow their movements. In this way, the complexities of dolphin society and the details of the dolphins' life histories are revealed. *Top left:* The ancient Greeks celebrated dolphins by painting them on the walls of the palace at Knossos, on the island of Crete. This painter had either seen wild dolphins or was familiar with the works of Aristotle, the first biologist who went to sea and studied dolphins. They look like striped dolphins, one of the two main species that frequent these waters today. The others are common dolphins, *bottom left*, playfully swimming in the classic dolphin pose as they approach a ship to bow-ride.

on dolphins are likely true; in recent years, children, as well as adults, have ridden dolphins along the shores of the United States, Ireland, France, Spain, Yugoslavia, Australia and Great Britain. Dolphins have also been known to support drowning swimmers and nudge them to shore. However, there are several documented cases of dolphins pushing people *away* from safety and butting them or holding them underwater. No wild dolphin is known to have killed a person. Yet dolphins are strong, independent animals that must be respected at all times.

Rather than striving to give these fascinating sociable mammals human status or confining them to the realm of the divine, though, we should appreciate that the ways of dolphins are uniquely their own.

SWIMMING AND DIVING

Hundreds of common dolphins skim the sea, making low-angle leaps across the waves, perhaps to reduce drag and build up speed. Displays such as this occur when herds of common dolphins are travelling. The birds overhead are a sign that the dolphins are feeding near the surface. The dolphins' frenetic activity causes the fish to panic and form tight schools, where they become easy targets for the dolphins—and the birds.

Dolphins and porpoises are fast swimmers, and many species are outstanding deep divers. To land mammals like us, their routines are astonishing feats. Orcas, pantropical spotted dolphins and northern right whale dolphins are among the fastest species, yet each achieves speed with different body and fin shapes. Their bodies vary from the bulky orca, which weighs up to 5,000 kilograms, to the lithe 70-kilogram northern right whale dolphin. An orca dorsal fin can be 1.8 metres high, while the broad flippers are up to 2 metres long, almost one-quarter of the average orca's body length; the northern right whale dolphin has small flippers and no dorsal fin at all. At high speed, a dorsal fin may help provide stability, but it also adds drag. All three species use strong tail muscles for propulsion and, com-

pared with humans, are streamlined.

Northern right whale dolphins have been clocked at 40 kilometres per hour and can sustain speeds of 25 kilometres per hour for up to 30 minutes. As they skim the water with their low-angle leaps, they can cover seven metres before they reenter the water and burst out again. Together with the absence of a dorsal fin, this technique allows them to avoid drag and to achieve greater speeds.

In one experiment, pantropical spotted dolphins trained to chase a lure accelerated to a top speed of 11 metres per second in just two seconds. For short speed bursts, the maximum power output was 50 percent greater per unit of body weight than that of human athletes. Orcas, estimated to travel at speed bursts of up to 48 kilometres per hour, may be the fastest of the dolphins.

How deep dolphins and porpoises dive depends on the availability of food. Because some fish live only at certain depths, scientists can sometimes tell where dolphins feed by examining the stomachs of dead dolphins and identifying fish remains.

Dolphins were trained in one experiment to trip switches on a submarine cable to indicate the depth of dive. One bottlenose dolphin repeatedly dived almost 300 metres and stayed down for 5 minutes. Pilot whales have reached 600 metres on 16-minute dives. The record dolphin dive belongs to an orca off Alaska that became entangled in telegraph cable at a depth of 1,030 metres.

Unlike large whales, most dolphins do not migrate with the seasons. Yet they often travel great distances in a day, mainly in search of food. By staying on the move, dolphins never eliminate a food source by eating all the fish or squid in one area. Many prey species keep moving as well, and dolphins follow them. Pilot whales seem to track the movements of squid, while common dolphins trail various fish that sometimes swim hundreds of kilometres.

Food may not be the only reason dolphins and porpoises move, though. In some seas, spinner dolphins and certain porpoises seem to enter shallow waters to avoid attack by sharks or orcas. And dolphins that form all-male or all-female groups must set out eventually in search of mates.

The distance travelled varies by species, time of day and season. Spinner dolphins around Hawaii range up to 50 kilometres a day. They feed close to the coast during daylight hours but move offshore at night to feed in deep waters. Resident orcas off Vancouver Island may venture 120 to 160 kilometres a day in summer when salmon are swimming in great schools from the open sea to the rivers. In winter, food supplies are even more dispersed, and orcas spread out over larger areas.

Coastal bottlenose dolphins have home ranges that vary according to gender and age. In Sarasota Bay, Florida, females with calves have the largest and most productive home ranges – about 40 square kilometres.

Nursing females require the most food. The males, meanwhile, have to roam over less productive areas.

River dolphins and some porpoises have much smaller home ranges. Generally restricted to rivers, a few river dolphins move out into the open sea. Harbour porpoises in the Bay of Fundy have been followed for a four-day period, during which they travelled 40 kilometres. The longest distance covered in one day was 20 kilometres, while the average was 10 kilometres – less than 10 percent of the distance some orcas traverse. In winter, many harbour porpoises in this area move offshore, presumably to enjoy the warmer waters touched by the Gulf Stream.

Like land mammals and birds, many dolphins and porpoises have home ranges to which they return year after year. These ranges are not considered territories. To qualify as a territory, an area must be defended – either from other species or from members of the same species. There is as yet no evidence that dolphins and porpoises use aggression to maintain exclusive use of a habitat.

Orcas off Vancouver Island, British Columbia, can be tracked with suction-cup radio tags. The movements of resident orcas here are relatively well known, but transient pods, such as these individuals from O pod and M pod, are sometimes seen only once or twice a year. Where do they go? Are their living patterns different from those of the residents? Through radio-tagging, researchers working with Robin W. Baird are learning more about the transients. The radio transmitter signals when the whale surfaces. From such signals, the researchers can determine the location of the whale and how long it has stayed down. Regular patterns of submerging and surfacing indicate travelling or resting; irregular patterns are often a sign of hunting activity. Transients travel along much of the B.C. coast, but one day, we may be able to track their movements at sea.

Found in the western Pacific and Indian oceans, finless porpoises resemble other porpoises in size, but their light colouring and lack of dorsal fin are unique. Like other porpoises, they inhabit coastal waters and sometimes ascend rivers, forming resident populations in such places as the Yangtze River in China. Because they live close to humans, porpoises around the world are threatened by pollution, fishing nets and ship traffic. In some areas, they have disappeared entirely, permanently displaced by humans and their activities.

The true porpoises are the cetaceans nearest in size to humans. An average adult harbour porpoise, for example, is 1.5 metres long and weighs 54 to 65 kilograms; a few reach 1.8 metres and 90 kilograms. At sea, however, this animal seems much smaller. On the surface of the water, only the dorsal fin and occasionally the head and back are visible. Porpoises travel in groups of fewer than 10. If you don't watch carefully or listen for their quick "puffs" at the surface, you will miss them altogether.

Most porpoises live close to shore, although an exception is the Dall's porpoise, which is found just as often in the open sea.

Next to river dolphins, porpoises are the most threatened cetaceans. They have suffered significant losses as a result of their inevitable conflict with human activities. In an apparent effort to avoid pollution or too much shipping traffic, porpoises have relocated, leaving some areas permanently. Nevertheless, thousands of porpoises drown every year in fishing nets, and many kills go unreported. When fishermen haul up a dead porpoise in their nets, they simply cut it out and toss it back into the sea.

Compared with the high-profile dolphins and whales, porpoises have as yet been unable to attract the wide public concern that is crucial to conservation efforts. As a result, they have been mostly overlooked in terms of research funding and protection. But porpoises have yet another strike against them: their small size makes it difficult for researchers to obtain the essential identification photographs to use in their studies.

With their striking black-and-white colouring, Dall's porpoises are sometimes mistaken for baby orcas, yet their behaviour is dramatically different. Compared with orcas, Dall's porpoises are hyperactive, moving so fast that most photographs of them are blurred. Sometimes, they surround a boat, bow-riding, but their rooster-tail splashes obscure the back and dorsal fin. An encounter lasts a few seconds, then they're gone.

At up to 2.2 metres long and 220 kilograms, Dall's porpoises are the largest of the true porpoises. They are also the most like dolphins in their social habits. Ranging offshore and along the coasts in the North Pacific, they sometimes travel in dolphin-sized herds of up to 3,000. They have colonized literally the whole temperate North Pacific, and recent population estimates range from a few hundred thousand to more than two million.

Over the past few decades, however, Dall's porpoises have been killed in great numbers, mainly by Japanese fishermen. Salmon gill-netters using drift nets are accidentally snaring and killing thousands. In Japanese waters, fishermen harpoon the porpoises by hand from boats and small ships. Between 1986 and 1989, the number of recorded catches was more than 110,000. Population estimates for this area are not much higher.

Phocoenoides dalli
Size: 1.8 to 2.2 metres; 135 to 220 kilograms.
Calves at birth: 85 to 100 centimetres.
Teeth: 19 to 28 teeth on each side of upper and lower jaws.
Food: Fish (capelin, Pacific hake, Pacific and jack mackerel, sardines, blennies and herring) and squid.
Habitat: Deep water and close to shore.
Range: Cooler waters of the North Pacific and Bering Sea.
Status: Population unknown, but at least in the hundreds of thousands.

A school of harbour porpoises races through the water, their glossy, dark, triangular dorsal fins flashing, then disappearing. On the move, these porpoises surface six to eight times a minute to breathe. When feeding, they surface only about once a minute. Compared with dolphins, harbour porpoises are all business, rarely performing the acrobatic feats of dolphins. As Aristotle long ago noted, porpoises do not have the dolphin "smile" and look almost "gloomy."

Of the six species classified by scientists as true porpoises, the harbour porpoise has the widest range and is the most commonly seen. Preferring cooler waters, it lives along the coasts of northern North America, Europe and northeastern Asia. Its near-shore habits, however, make the species vulnerable to shipping traffic, pollution and entanglement in fishing gear.

Much of what is known about harbour porpoises can be traced to the early work of David E. Gaskin, a British biologist based at the University of Guelph, in Ontario, Canada. In 1969, Gaskin set up a field station on the Bay of Fundy in New Brunswick to conduct studies of porpoise biology and ecology. From shore and from ferries and other boats, he monitored the porpoises year after year as they moved through the island passages.

Gaskin and his students found that most of the harbour porpoises arrive in the Bay of Fundy in spring, soon after the water temperature reaches 8 degrees C. Females with newborn calves arrive in mid-July. The population peaks in August and stays until September or mid-October. In autumn and winter, the porpoises are few and far between. In rain, snow or fog, it is nearly impossible to see them.

Gaskin says the porpoises' seasonal movements seem to follow those of their main prey, herring and mackerel. Sometimes, he watched them chasing speedy mackerel near the surface – the one brief occasion when the porpoises abandon their shy manner – swimming up to 22 kilometres per hour as they dashed through the water in mad pursuit. Gaskin and his students examined the stomachs of dead porpoises to learn what they eat: cephalopods and a variety of fish (herring, mackerel, pollack, silver hake and whiting). Harbour porpoises seem to prefer schooling, nonspiny fish.

Farther south, in the Gulf of Maine, right whale researchers led by Scott Kraus from the New England Aquarium have also studied harbour por-

Phocoena phocoena
Size: 1.4 to 1.8 metres; 54 to 65 kilograms. Females slightly larger than males.
Calves at birth: 67 to 80 centimetres.
Teeth: 19 to 28 small, spade-shaped teeth on each side of upper and lower jaws.
Food: Fish (especially bottom fish, herring, mackerel, whiting and anchovies).
Habitat: Mainly coastal.
Range: Temperate and subarctic North Atlantic and Pacific plus Black Sea and Sea of Azov.
Status: Population unknown.

poises. In July 1982, in the first Gulf of Maine census, they estimated that there were at least 8,000 harbour porpoises. Some 3,000 more were thought to be in Canadian waters in the Bay of Fundy. After the census, the researchers began to suspect that the Gulf of Maine/Bay of Fundy harbour porpoises formed a distinct population. Staying in the area from spring through autumn, they then moved offshore in winter – perhaps to the edge of the continental shelf or the Grand Banks and Georges Bank.

Gaskin, Kraus and others have worried about threats to porpoises, especially the danger of their getting caught in gill nets. The porpoises suffocate when they cannot surface to breathe. At first, the number of deaths seemed low – fewer than 15 a year were reported in the Bay of Fundy in the early 1980s. But some fishermen do not make the reports that the law requires. Later research has shown that during the late 1980s, probably 600 to 1,000 a year were killed.

Furthermore, Gaskin and his associate Andrew Read have found fewer small calves and large females in recent years, a sign that the killings are having a damaging effect on the population and may be reducing its reproductive potential. Harbour porpoises have a low reproductive rate. A female can produce only two or three calves in her lifetime, which is an average of 7 to 8 years.

Gaskin and Read are working to control the use of gill nets and trying to make nets more visible to the porpoises. Stiffer American regulations are also necessary in the Gulf of Maine. Many conservationists think that gill nets should be outlawed.

Harbour porpoises have been well studied off California, around Denmark and in the Black Sea, yet their conservation needs are neglected. "They are small," says Kraus, and today, no one catches them for food or other products. "They have no value except to those of us who like them and enjoy seeing them in the wild."

A brief glimpse of a black dorsal fin, *far left*, is all that is usually seen of a harbour porpoise. If seas are a little rough, the low, triangular fin is not visible at all. Because harbour porpoises are difficult to observe, photo-identification methods have not yet been attempted. Like other porpoise populations that live close to humans in the North Atlantic and in the Pacific, harbour porpoise numbers have declined as pollution, fishing and ship traffic have increased.

VAQUITA

Inhabiting only the northern Gulf of California in Mexican waters, the vaquita is probably the most mysterious and elusive of all dolphins and porpoises. Although the species was discovered in 1958, few scientists have ever seen a vaquita – dead or alive. Researchers studying vaquitas even have trouble finding them.

One scientist searched for 15 days and had just three sightings. In the early 1980s, two scientific expeditions – each ranging over almost 2,000 kilometres – resulted in three "probable sightings." Finally, fearing that the vaquita was virtually extinct, researcher Greg Silber spent four seasons between 1986 and 1989 combing the northern gulf. In boat and aerial surveys covering 4,216 kilometres, he logged 110 sightings. This is a small number considering the effort. Yet it does suggest that a few hundred individuals remain.

We know little about the vaquita's life history and habits. It is thought to live in small groups of 2 to 4, perhaps 10 at most. The stomach contents of one revealed a diet of fish that are abundant in the upper gulf. Each year, some 30 to 40 are killed in fishing nets and shrimp trawls – not a huge number but a perilous one for an endangered species. Only if we can save this elusive animal is there any chance we can learn more about it.

Phocoena sinus
Size: 1.2 to 1.5 metres; 30 to 55 kilograms. Females slightly larger than males.
Calves at birth: Unknown.
Teeth: 20 to 21 small, spade-shaped teeth on each side of upper jaw and 18 teeth on each side of lower jaw.
Food: Fish (grunts, gulf croakers) and squid.
Habitat: Coastal.
Range: Far northern Gulf of California, Mexico.
Status: Endangered. Population unknown but very small, perhaps low hundreds.

The finless porpoise is the only porpoise without a dorsal fin. Because the dorsal fin is often used in photo-identification studies, the absence of one makes research in the wild difficult. The dorsal fin also helps observers locate the animals at sea. To identify a finless porpoise, researchers must either watch carefully for its spout or move in very close. In addition, the porpoise is fairly small – less than two metres long – and usually travels in pairs. Occasionally, groups of 5 to 10 animals have been seen.

Finless porpoises are the only porpoises that live in the waters of tropical and warm temperate Asia.

More common than coastal dolphins throughout much of their range, they are found from the Persian Gulf, across southern Asia to Indonesia and north along China to Japan, where their numbers are also threatened by Japanese fishermen. They live in rivers and along coasts, favouring areas where fresh water meets the sea, such as estuaries and mangroves. Although they live in the Yangtze River in far greater numbers than the baiji, their preferred habitats are near some of the world's most densely populated areas. The pollution problems there make the prospects for the finless porpoise uncertain in many regions.

Neophocaena phocaenoides
Size: 1.4 to 1.9 metres; 30 to 45 kilograms. Males slightly larger than females.
Calves at birth: 80 centimetres.
Teeth: 13 to 22 partly spade-shaped teeth on each side of upper and lower jaws.
Food: Squid, sepias, shrimp and small fish.
Habitat: Coastal waters, estuaries and rivers.
Range: Tropical and temperate waters of the Indian Ocean, South China Sea and western North Pacific.
Status: Population unknown.

A baiji, *above*, cracks the surface of China's Yangtze River. The species is confined to the middle and lower reaches by the dredging of river channels and by dams built for flood prevention. To save the baiji, fishing regulations must be enforced. About half of all deaths occur when baijis become entangled in fishing gear, especially the illegal lines set with hooks to snag bottom fish. The boto, *above right*, has tiny eyes, a bulbous forehead and a long beak. Its ghostlike appearance as it looms out of the dark Amazonian waters makes it easy to understand why the boto became a creature of legend. Native people believed that botos possessed the souls of the drowned.

River dolphins are adapted to fresh water and are therefore able to live mainly in rivers. While not very streamlined, their bodies are flexible and are ideal for chasing prey in sometimes narrow, cramped river channels. Hunting singly or in small groups of two or three, river dolphins feed primarily on fish, including many slow-moving bottom species. Long rows of teeth help river dolphins grasp the fish; some have molarlike back teeth for crushing heavily armoured freshwater fish. Three river dolphin species are nearly blind, relying on echolocation to find food and to make their way through the murky river waters.

The most imperilled of all whales and dolphins, all but one of the five river dolphin species are considered "endangered" or "threatened." Each river dolphin has its own sad tale, but the stories are similar. Many of the world's rivers – dammed, overfished and polluted – simply have little remaining usable habitat.

In most of the countries in which river dolphins are found – China, India, Pakistan, Bangladesh and much of South America – greater numbers of people and their need for resources have added to the pressures on the rivers and surrounding land. Yet river dolphins survive partly because of the beliefs of the people who have lived alongside them. In China, the baiji was considered by some to be a princess, a creature of legend. In Brazil, the boto was spared because it was thought to be a sign of danger and misfortune. New settlers to the Amazon, however, do not share such respectful views.

The boto (BO-too) presents an odd sight, its pinkish body breaking the surface of the brown river waters of equatorial South America. The late Canadian scientist Robin Best and Brazilian scientist Vera da Silva lived among the elusive botos of the Brazilian Amazon for more than a decade, coming to know their habits and collecting stories about them.

While they rarely jump out of the water or lift their tails like other dolphins, botos can be playful, sometimes cavorting with river turtles and tossing them into the air. The researchers watched them throw sticks and play with logs, pull grass underwater, grab fishermen's paddles and rub against their canoes. Some fishermen even taught wild botos to herd and capture fish.

Slow-moving, botos lope along at about 1.5 to 3.2 kilometres per hour. In a sprint, they can briefly reach speeds of up to 14 kilometres per hour. Since they have to navigate the rapids in some of the upper-Amazon and Orinoco tributaries, botos are, by necessity, strong swimmers.

The boto's reputation is enhanced by legend and myth. In one story, the boto takes the form of a man and seduces unmarried girls with his captivating charm. In another, the dolphin becomes a mermaid, luring young men into the water.

Inia geoffrensis
Size: 2 to 2.5 metres; 85 to 160 kilograms.
Calves at birth: 70 to 83 centimetres.
Teeth: 24 to 34 teeth on each side of upper and lower jaws, with simple, conical teeth near the front and heavier, molar-type teeth in the back.
Food: Fish such as armoured catfish and at least 50 other species.
Habitat: Rivers.
Range: The Amazon and Orinoco river systems in Brazil, Venezuela, Colombia, Ecuador, Guyana, Peru and Bolivia.
Status: Vulnerable. Numbers unknown.

The baiji (BYE-chee) is the freshwater equivalent of a giant panda. Both are large, endangered mammals found only in China. Both are restricted to tiny parts of their former range. And both are attracting the serious efforts of scientists and conservationists from around the world who hope to save them. Despite being a "protected animal of the first order," the baiji is even more threatened and closer to extinction than the panda.

Baijis hunt in small groups of four or fewer, taking a wide variety of fish. The best hunting spots are near sandbanks and around the ends of islets or in areas where tributaries spill into the main river. Their white backs are barely visible as they glide to the surface. Occasionally, a long white beak will appear, but since they have poor vision, the animals have little reason to poke their heads out of the water to spyhop. After feeding, which takes place mainly in the early morning and at nightfall, baijis sometimes rest for up to six hours in the still centre of river eddies near the sandbanks.

With perhaps 300 or fewer remaining in the Yangtze River in central China, baijis are the river dolphins closest to extinction. Conservation plans currently under way include a semicaptive breeding programme in which two partly natural river reserves will be blocked off.

Lipotes vexillifer
Size: 2 to 2.5 metres; 135 to 230 kilograms. Females slightly larger than males.
Calves at birth: 70 to 80 centimetres.
Teeth: 30 to 35 conical teeth on each side of upper and lower jaws.
Food: Fish such as catfish and large-scaled fish.
Habitat: Rivers.
Range: Lower and middle Yangtze River system and adjacent lakes in China.
Status: Endangered. Close to extinction. Only 300 left and declining.

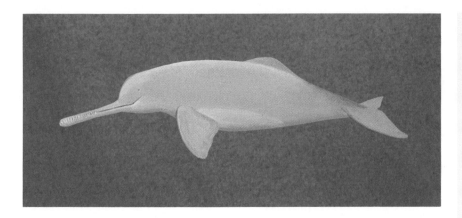

Platanista gangetica
Size: 2 to 2.5 metres; 80 to 90 kilograms. Females larger than males.
Calves at birth: 70 to 75 centimetres.
Teeth: 27 to 33 slender, sharp-pointed teeth on each side of upper and lower jaws.
Food: Fish (catfish), mollusks and crustaceans.
Habitat: Rivers.
Range: The Ganges, Brahmaputra, Karnaphuli and Meghna river systems from the foot of the Himalayas to the tidal zone in India, Bangladesh, Nepal and Bhutan.
Status: Vulnerable. Total population about 5,000.

For now, the Ganges susu plies the muddy waters of the Ganges, Karnaphuli and Brahmaputra river systems in India, Bangladesh, Bhutan and Nepal. But some 22 dams and barrages on the Ganges, with seven more being built, are dividing the populations into isolated fragments.

Platanista minor
Size: 2 to 2.5 metres; 80 to 90 kilograms. Females larger than males.
Calves at birth: 70 to 75 centimetres.
Teeth: 27 to 33 slender, sharp-pointed teeth on each side of upper and lower jaws.
Food: Fish (catfish), mollusks and crustaceans.
Habitat: Rivers.
Range: Indus River system within the provinces of Sind and Punjab, Pakistan.
Status: Endangered. Close to extinction. About 500 individuals left.

The bhulan (BOO-lang) is closely related to the Ganges susu. Some scientists think they may be the same species. It once ranged from the Himalayan foothills to the Arabian Sea but is now confined to Pakistan. With 500 animals left, the bhulan is almost as endangered as the baiji.

Oceanic dolphins are the animals most people picture when they hear the word dolphin. Yet dolphins include species like the bottlenose, *above*, as well as the dolphins with "whale" in their names, such as the short-finned pilot whale, *right*. Most oceanic dolphins are bigger than river dolphins or porpoises and range over comparatively larger areas of the world ocean, from near coastal regions to the open sea.

The most playful and acrobatic dolphins, these are the bow-riders and high leapers that have become famous both in marine parks and aquariums and in the wild.

By far the largest family of dolphins and porpoises, oceanic dolphins encompass more than two dozen species. Most oceanic dolphins spend their lives ranging over vast areas of the open sea, far from land. Many species are distributed throughout the world ocean. Others, like the porpoises, are mainly coastal. A few species occasionally swim up rivers, and some even live there permanently, side by side with true river dolphins.

Oceanic dolphins, typically larger than river dolphins or porpoises, vary a great deal in size. The tucuxi – smaller than most porpoises – is only 1.4 to 1.8 metres long and weighs 36 to 45 kilograms. The largest is the orca, or killer whale, which measures up to 9.8 metres and can weigh 5,000 kilograms, making it even bigger than certain whale species, such as beaked whales. The oceanic dolphins include six large dolphin species that have the word "whale" in their common name. Because of their size, they are sometimes treated as whales for management purposes.

The threats affecting oceanic dolphins vary by species. Those in coastal waters suffer many of the same problems that porpoises do: shore pollution, ship traffic and fishing nets. Open-ocean dolphins encounter less pollution, but some, such as spotted and spinner dolphins, face another hazard: because many travel with tuna, they are often ensnared in tuna nets, where they drown. Even more extensive and deadly are the deep-sea drift nets which trap and kill almost everything that swims into them. Until such nets are banned, many species of dolphins, as well as fish and other marine life, are at risk.

We do not really know the status of most oceanic dolphins. Many species are probably less endangered than river dolphins and porpoises, whose ranges are far more restricted. And even if a number of oceanic dolphin populations are threatened, groups of the same species in other areas may remain healthy.

Steno bredanensis
Size: 2.2 to 2.4 metres; 120 kilograms. Males slightly larger than females.
Calves at birth: Unknown.
Teeth: 20 to 27 teeth on each side of upper and lower jaws.
Food: Fish, deep-sea octopuses, squid and mollusks.
Habitat: Deep offshore waters.
Range: Tropical, subtropical and warm temperate world ocean.
Status: Population unknown.

In warm temperate and tropical waters, herds of up to 50 rough-toothed dolphins skim the open sea, although the average group size is only 6. Sometimes, they team up with pilot whales and bottlenose dolphins, probably diving for deep-sea squid, octopuses and fish.

TUCUXI

Sotalia fluviatilis
Size: 1.4 to 1.8 metres; 36 to 45 kilograms.
Calves at birth: 70 to 80 centimetres.
Teeth: 26 to 35 teeth on each side of upper and lower jaws; often raggedly arranged in lower jaw.
Food: Fish (armoured catfish) and crustaceans.
Habitat: Coastal waters, especially bays and rivers.
Range: Orinoco and Amazon river systems and coastal South Atlantic, from Panama to Santos, Brazil.
Status: Population unknown, but common throughout its range.

Travelling in groups of 2 to 25 individuals, the tucuxi (too-κοο-she) hunts near river channels, where turbulence disrupts fish schools. It is classified as an oceanic dolphin, though some live near the coast and others reside in the Amazon and Orinoco rivers of South America.

ATLANTIC HUMP-BACKED DOLPHIN

Like the tucuxi, the Atlantic hump-backed dolphin inhabits coastal waters and may ascend rivers, although its freshwater range is not well known. In some areas of the West African coast, it lives and feeds around the rich fish nurseries of the mangrove forests.

From October to December and February to May in the northwestern African country of Mauritania, Atlantic hump-backed dolphins take part in a cooperative effort to catch a fish called mullet. Their partners are not only bottlenose dolphins but also the villagers, who leave their homes to camp along the Bay d'Argun during mullet season. Entering the water on foot, the villagers dip hand nets into the water to catch passing fish.

Imitating the splash made by the jumping fish, the villagers hit the surface of the water with sticks. The noise and commotion attract the dolphins, which swim toward the shore, blocking the mullet's escape. As the mullet are driven into the fishermen's nets, both dolphins and fishermen harvest a bounty of fish.

The villagers are grateful to the dolphins, although those which strand or die accidentally are used for food or oil. The people of Mauritania and nearby Senegal, where the species is also found, need every food source they can find to survive.

Sousa teuszii
Size: 2 metres; 100 kilograms.
Calves at birth: Unknown.
Teeth: 26 to 31 peglike teeth on each side of upper and lower jaws.
Food: Fish (mullet) and crustaceans.
Habitat: Coastal waters.
Range: Off West Africa, from Mauritania south to Cameroon and perhaps Angola.
Status: Population unknown.

Friends of the ancient Romans and Greeks and immortalized by Aristotle, common dolphins were sometimes caught by Mediterranean fishermen, who nicked their tails and released them. According to Aristotle, the nicks allowed the fishermen to identify individuals if they were caught again.

The fishermen might have had more luck identifying the dolphins by nicking their dorsal fins rather than their tails. One thing, though, is clear: the Greeks felt a decided affection for dolphins and regarded their appearance as a good omen.

In many ways, the common dolphin – with its classic slender, streamlined silhouette and long black beak – is the model dolphin. Found throughout the world ocean, members of this species are fast, active swimmers and enthusiastic jumpers and bow-riders, ever eager to practise typical dolphin behaviour. Finally, they are highly social, travelling in herds of dozens to hundreds or more.

On the feeding banks, the common dolphin can be seen with Pacific white-sided dolphins in the Pacific and with many other species of dolphins in the Atlantic. As wide-ranging as this dolphin is, however, certain populations are threatened. Many are killed annually when they are accidentally netted by fishermen.

Delphinus delphis
Size: 1.7 to 2.4 metres; 75 to 85 kilograms. Males slightly larger than females.
Calves at birth: 79 to 90 centimetres.
Teeth: 40 to 55, sometimes up to 58, small, sharp-pointed teeth on each side of upper and lower jaws.
Food: Fish (various cod, hake and pilchards) and squid.
Habitat: Mainly offshore waters.
Range: Tropical, subtropical and warm temperate world ocean, including Mediterranean, Red and Black seas and Persian Gulf.
Status: Population unknown. Declines noted in some areas, but common in most parts of its range.

Along the coast of the southeastern United States and Baja California, Mexico, dolphins have been seen charging toward the shore, literally chasing fish out of the water. In hot pursuit of its prey, the dolphin beaches itself, grabs a fish in its beak, then wriggles back into the water.

Individual dolphins along the British, Irish, American and Australian coasts regularly allow people to approach, taking them for rides through the water and sometimes presenting them with gifts of live fish.

Off Hawaii and the U.S. east coast, trained dolphins perform military test manoeuvres in the open sea, while in the Persian Gulf, they are reported to have searched for mines.

In the Caribbean, off Hawaii and wherever large whales such as humpbacks gather, dolphins can be found, swimming circles around the whales and stealing rides by coasting beside them and bow-riding in the pressure waves they create. On the tropical mating grounds, they linger near the humpback singers, perhaps enjoying the concert.

This astonishing variety of behaviour provides but a brief glimpse of the versatile, infinitely adaptable bottlenose dolphin. More than any other dolphin, the bottlenose forms long-term associations with such widely different species as sea turtles, humpback whales and humans. But the intimate patterns of daily dolphin life change from place to place, from day to day and from individual to individual. So varied is this dolphin's behaviour that it is sometimes difficult to determine patterns at all.

The bottlenose dolphin is the species most familiar to humans, because it has been shown in aquariums since the 1860s. Its apparent adaptability to captive life has proved valuable for researchers. More than 100 bottlenose dolphins have been born in aquariums, and some of those calves have matured, mated and themselves given birth in captivity.

Much of what we know about the social life of all dolphins is the result of studies of wild bottlenose dolphin societies. In the early 1970s, researchers Randall Wells, Michael Scott and Blair Irvine began to visit the bottle-nose dolphin population living in the shallow bays off the west coast of Florida, near Sarasota. Using photographs, they identified each animal and, at times, tagged and radio-tracked them. When the scientists could recognize individual dolphins, they were able to define the population and the social groupings and to monitor the comings and goings of the members. The researchers also captured known individuals, took blood samples for genetic analysis, then released the dolphins. From such studies, we have learned:

The bottlenose dolphins that live around Sarasota form a relatively stable unit of about 100 individuals. This

population has its own home range but shares its borders with other bottlenose dolphin communities. The older males, in particular, live along the borders and visit back and forth. In this way, there is some genetic mixing between adjacent groups, which is healthy for the population. Still, most social interactions occur within each community.

Mothers and their calves develop strong bonds that last three to six years, long past the estimated weaning age of 18 to 20 months. Young male and female adults swim in mixed subgroups. Males, however, gradually form their own buddy groups. Two or three males of the same age may stay together into adulthood – sometimes for life. Young females, meanwhile, travel with other sub-adults until they calve at 8 to 12 years of age. Then they join bands of adult females and their young.

In the Sarasota community, there are three of these bands, each composed mainly of related females that remain in the same core area. The adult males – either alone or in buddy pairs or trios – move from one band to another and occasionally visit bands in other communities.

A rich overall picture of a bottlenose dolphin community is emerging from the life histories of so many individuals. Some animals, whose teeth have been examined for growth layers, are known to be in their late forties. To learn more about these and other bottlenose dolphin communities simply requires time and clever

strategies that will allow us to study the dolphins with minimal disturbance to their lives.

Research on the social behaviour of dolphins is also being conducted off the coasts of Texas, California, Portugal, Great Britain, Western Australia, Chile, South Africa and Argentina, among other areas. While these studies confirm many of the Florida findings, each has revealed some tantalizing new information. Off Western Australia, for example, the bottlenose dolphins have become so tame that it is possible to approach them in small boats and even to wade among them in shallow water. Such observations have begun to unlock the mysteries of how dolphins form friendships with each other and compete for mates.

What we know about the "mind" of the dolphin comes from these studies

A bottlenose dolphin breaches high in the air, *left*, while three bottlenose dolphins demonstrate their remarkable hunting manoeuvres, *above*. The dolphins have driven fish onto the shore, then beached themselves to retrieve their prey. After grabbing the fish, the dolphins wriggle back into the water. Such behaviour is common along the South Carolina/Georgia coast, where this photograph was taken, as well as off the west coast of Baja California, Mexico, in the Pacific.

BOTTLENOSE DOLPHIN

– particularly those concerning bottlenose dolphin individuals kept captive as part of scientific programmes, for military research and as aquarium performers. Our research findings on dolphin communication, courtship, mating and motherhood are, for the most part, courtesy of the cooperative nature of bottlenose dolphins.

Yet the benefits of a close association between humans and bottlenose dolphins may prove to be tragically one-sided. Along the east coast of the United States, from New Jersey to Florida, roughly 750 bottlenose dolphins washed up dead in late 1987 and early 1988. Researchers determined that a number of factors had led to a weakening of the dolphins' immune systems and their eventual deaths, including red-tide toxins and possibly contaminants such as PCBs picked up in fish they had eaten. Meanwhile, the offshore bottlenose dolphins, a separate population, were apparently unaffected.

Aquarium performer, occasional wild companion to humans, source of inspiration – the bottlenose is a high-profile, cosmopolitan dolphin. Its adaptiveness as a species has made it successful around the world. While the bottlenose dolphin may be unable to articulate the threat to its habitat, its presence remains one of the best monitors of the health of our shores.

Tursiops truncatus
Size: 2.3 to 3.1 metres; 150 to 275 kilograms. Males larger than females.
Calves at birth: 98 to 130 centimetres.
Teeth: 18 to 26 teeth on each side of upper and lower jaws.
Food: Fish (mullet, anchovies, herring, cod, menhaden and a wide variety of other species) and squid.
Habitat: Mainly coastal but also offshore waters.
Range: World ocean except polar seas.
Status: Population unknown. Declines noted in some areas, but common in most parts of its range.

Stenella attenuata
Size: 1.9 to 2.3 metres; 110 kilograms. Males slightly larger than females, and coastal slightly larger than offshore dolphins.
Calves at birth: 82.5 to 89 centimetres.
Teeth: 29 to 34 small, sharp-pointed teeth on each side of upper jaw; 33 to 36 teeth on each side of lower jaw.
Food: Fish (anchovies, herring and others) and squid.
Habitat: Mainly offshore.
Range: Tropical and subtropical waters of the world ocean.
Status: Population unknown, but common in most parts of its range. Substantial declines have occurred in the eastern tropical Pacific.

In the eastern tropical Pacific, herds of up to several thousand spotted and spinner dolphins travel with seabirds overhead and schools of yellowfin tuna below. Using helicopters to locate the dolphins, tuna fishing fleets exploit this situation, and many dolphins suffocate in their nets.

SPINNER DOLPHIN

Stenella longirostris
Size: 1.7 to 2.2 metres; 75 kilograms. Males slightly larger than females.
Calves at birth: 77 centimetres.
Teeth: 45 to 65 sharp-pointed teeth on each side of upper and lower jaws.
Food: Fish (small deep-ocean species) and squid.
Habitat: Mainly offshore.
Range: Tropical, subtropical and warm temperate world ocean.
Status: Population unknown, but common in most parts of its range. Substantial declines have occurred in the eastern tropical Pacific.

So called for their high, spinning leaps, spinner dolphins are known as playful, eager bow-riders throughout much of their range. But in the eastern tropical Pacific, where tuna fishermen have killed millions of spinners since 1959, the dolphins no longer approach ships.

STRIPED DOLPHIN

With their elegantly "painted" face masks and delicate features, striped dolphins were appreciated for their beauty by the ancient Greeks. They appear on classical frescoes looking much as they do today swimming through the Mediterranean Sea. Because of the large size of their herds as well as their acrobatic behaviour, they are easy to identify when they move through an area.

Despite their beauty, striped dolphins have been killed in large numbers in recent years. Among the agents of death are: viruses and possibly pollution in the Mediterranean; nets used to catch fish in the tropical Pacific; and dolphin hunting around Japan.

Striped dolphins are still considered common throughout their range, but more research is needed.

In the Pacific, striped dolphins form five kinds of schools, or groups: adult breeding; adult nonbreeding; mixed breeding; mixed nonbreeding; and juvenile. The schools are constantly changing. In the adult breeding school, males often leave after mating. It then becomes an adult nonbreeding school. When calves are born, it turns into a mixed nonbreeding school. One to two years after weaning, calves form juvenile schools. As juveniles reach sexual maturity, first females, then males are accepted into adult breeding or nonbreeding schools.

Stenella coeruleoalba
Size: 2.1 to 2.4 metres; 100 kilograms. Males slightly larger than females.
Calves at birth: 100 centimetres.
Teeth: 45 to 50 slightly in-curved teeth on each side of upper and lower jaws.
Food: Fish (various cod) and squid.
Habitat: Mainly offshore.
Range: Tropical, subtropical and warm temperate world ocean.
Status: Population unknown, but common throughout its range.

In the Bahamas, Denise Herzing and other researchers spend part of every year with some 50 Atlantic spotted dolphins. Underwater viewing with video cameras allows them to identify individuals by examining the dorsal fin, fluke marks and "constellations" of spots. Researchers can estimate ages by observing the size of the dolphin and the patterns on its body. These change from two-toned in calves to speckled in juveniles, mottled in young adults and fused, or fully spotted, in older adults. Researchers can tell their sex and determine which females are pregnant by looking for a slight bulge in the midsection.

Through such studies, we have discovered that the dolphins form long-term bonds and learn, as young calves, by doing things with their mothers and other dolphins. A calf nurses for up to three years, although it practises chasing and catching bottom fish before 6 months of age. At 3 to 5 years, it leaves its mother when she gives birth to another calf. The juvenile joins a group of the same sex for four or five years. These juveniles, sometimes supervised by an adult, go on hunting expeditions but typically stay on the sidelines, watching. A youngster occasionally returns to its mother to interact with her and her new calf. The females mature at age 6 or more, the males at about age 15.

Stenella frontalis
Size: 1.8 to 2.2 metres; 110 kilograms.
Calves at birth: 88 to 120 centimetres.
Teeth: 29 to 34 small, sharp-pointed teeth on each side of upper jaw; 33 to 36 teeth on each side of lower jaw.
Food: Various small fish species and squid.
Habitat: Mainly offshore waters, sometimes coastal.
Range: Tropical, subtropical and warm temperate Atlantic.
Status: Population unknown.

CLYMENE DOLPHIN

Stenella clymene
Size: 1.8 to 2 metres; 75 kilograms.
Calves at birth: Unknown.
Teeth: 38 to 49 sharp-pointed teeth on each side of upper and lower jaws.
Food: Small fish and squid.
Habitat: Deep offshore waters.
Range: Tropical, subtropical and warm temperate Atlantic.
Status: Population unknown.

The clymene (cly-MEE-nee) dolphin is closely related to and can be confused with the spinner dolphin. It is sometimes called the short-snouted spinner dolphin. It, too, spins when it leaps out of the water, but the leaps are neither as high nor as spectacular as the spinner's.

FRASER'S DOLPHIN

Lagenodelphis hosei
Size: 2.3 to 2.5 metres; 160 to 210 kilograms.
Calves at birth: 100 centimetres.
Teeth: 34 to 44 slender, pointed teeth on each side of upper and lower jaws.
Food: Fish (various cod), small squid and crustaceans.
Habitat: Deep offshore waters.
Range: Tropical waters of the world ocean.
Status: Population unknown.

The Fraser's dolphin was once thought to be rare. For decades, the species was identified only from the remains of a single skeleton. Since the early 1970s, however, schools of up to 1,000 Fraser's dolphins have been seen plying the deep waters of the tropical ocean.

Whale-watching tours to offshore California waters have introduced many people to herds of Pacific white-sided dolphins. In the late 1980s, researcher Nancy Black of Moss Landing Marine Laboratories in California began an intensive study to learn more about this lively dolphin.

Typical group size, according to Black, is 30 or fewer, especially when the dolphins are feeding and socializing. When travelling or resting, though, they sometimes swim in herds of several hundred to a thousand or more. They often keep company with northern right whale dolphins, Risso's dolphins and, occasionally, bottlenose dolphins and California sea lions. Using the technique of radio tracking, Black has found that Pacific white-sided dolphins are probably daytime feeders.

Within the large, scattered groups, Black has tried to photograph "white" Pacific white-sided dolphins — mainly white individuals that have distinctive markings — as well as others with nicks on their dorsal fins. She calls such individuals "herd markers" and has reidentified them up to five times, finding that some white-sided dolphins spend from early summer to early winter in the offshore Monterey Bay, California, area. From January through May, the dolphins move farther offshore or to other areas.

Lagenorhynchus obliquidens
Size: 1.9 to 2.3 metres; 150 kilograms. Males slightly larger than females.
Calves at birth: 102 to 124 centimetres.
Teeth: 21 to 28 small, pointed, slightly curved teeth on each side of upper and lower jaws.
Food: Fish (anchovies, hake and pilchards) and small squid.
Habitat: Mainly off the continental shelf to deep offshore waters.
Range: Temperate North Pacific.
Status: Population unknown.

In the northern Gulf of St. Lawrence, off Québec, Richard Sears and his Mingan Island Cetacean Study team often encounter Atlantic white-sided dolphins and white-beaked dolphins. In mixed herds up to 200 strong, the dolphins sweep across a whitecapped sea on their feeding runs, jumping and lobtailing in a flurry of flying spray. In the middle of the herd swim humpback and fin whales and sometimes minke and blue whales. It is one of the great North American marine wildlife parades.

Atlantic white-sided dolphins and white-beaked dolphins are approachable and curious, although some books have claimed that the white-beaked dolphin is shy. From time to time, both species will ride the bows of boats. Like dolphins in many parts of the world, the Gulf of St. Lawrence dolphins often stay close to the larger whales and at times socialize with and even bother them. Using close-up camera work, Sears has documented the presence of tooth marks and scars on the fins of the whales that could have been made only by dolphins. It is difficult to say why dolphins would bite a whale, but maybe they regard it as a potential member of the school and are just testing or evaluating it.

Atlantic white-sided and white-beaked dolphins are closely related,

Lagenorhynchus acutus
Size: 2.3 to 2.5 metres; 165 kilograms. Males slightly larger than females.
Calves at birth: 110 centimetres.
Teeth: 29 to 40 small, sharp-pointed teeth on each side of upper and lower jaws.
Food: Fish (herring, cod, mackerel, hake and others), squid and crustaceans.
Habitat: Mainly offshore waters.
Range: Temperate and subpolar waters of North Atlantic.
Status: Population unknown, but probably tens of thousands to low hundreds of thousands.

belonging to the same genus, *Lagenorhynchus*. In the outports of Newfoundland, fishermen call the white-beaked "squidhound" and the Atlantic white-sided "jumper." In fact, both eat squid as well as fish, and both are good jumpers. They live in the cooler temperate waters of the North Atlantic, and their ranges overlap. Yet a student of wild whales will note certain differences. The white-beaked dolphin seems to prefer more northerly waters and can be seen swimming at the edge of the polar ice.

How do Sears and his team distinguish the two species when dolphins sometimes swim together in herds of 500 to 1,000 or more? The animal's white beak is usually difficult to see underwater. To make matters more confusing, some white-beaked dolphins have black beaks, just like Atlantic white-sided dolphins. Researchers have found that the best clue for identifying the white-beaked dolphin is the white patch on its side, just below the dorsal fin, that continues back and up onto the saddle, the area directly behind the dorsal fin. By contrast, the Atlantic white-sided dolphin has a white patch on the side below the dorsal fin that goes straight back and turns into bright yellow or tan. Even on a cloudy day, with the dolphins skimming through the sea, the yellow patch seems to glow.

Lagenorhynchus albirostris
Size: 2.5 to 2.7 metres; 180 kilograms. Males slightly larger than females.
Calves at birth: 120 centimetres.
Teeth: 22 to 28 small, sharp-pointed teeth on each side of upper and lower jaws.
Food: Fish (herring, cod, mackerel, whiting, haddock and others), squid, octopuses and crustaceans.
Habitat: Mainly offshore.
Range: Temperate and subpolar waters of North Atlantic.
Status: Population unknown, but probably tens of thousands to low hundreds of thousands.

NORTHERN RIGHT WHALE DOLPHIN

This smooth-backed dolphin presents a slim, graceful silhouette as it travels through the waters of the temperate North Pacific. Moving in great herds of several hundred to several thousand and leaping at low angles, northern right whale dolphins look like black crescents skimming the water. Occasionally, there are flashes of white from their brilliant belly patches. Their herds look completely unlike any other dolphin herd.

Northern right whale dolphins live far offshore and feed primarily on squid and deep-sea fish. They often form larger herds with several other dolphin species, especially Pacific white-sided dolphins. Generally, they avoid humans and rarely ride on the bow waves of ships. Researchers have watched them bunch together, then jet away from boats. At such times, making seven-metre shallow leaps to avoid drag, they have reached speeds of 40 kilometres per hour and sustained 25 kilometres per hour for half-hour periods.

Some northern right whale dolphins, along with other small whales and dolphins, have been hunted for food by the Japanese. Many more are killed accidentally in drift nets, particularly those set for squid. Despite these ongoing assaults on its numbers, however, the species appears to be fairly common.

Lissodelphis borealis
Size: 2.1 to 3.1 metres; 70 kilograms.
Calves at birth: 80 to 100 centimetres.
Teeth: 36 to 49 small, pointed teeth on each side of upper and lower jaws.
Food: Squid and many deep-sea fish species.
Habitat: Deep offshore waters.
Range: Temperate North Pacific.
Status: Population unknown, but common within its range.

The adult Risso's dolphin has all the markings of a battle veteran. Numerous white scars and scratches along its greyish flanks are evidence of extensive mouthing play or perhaps aggressive behaviour between adults. It may be a good thing that the adult Risso's dolphin has so few teeth – two to seven pairs – and those only in the lower jaw.

While Risso's dolphins travel in herds averaging 15 to 46 animals in tropical and warm temperate seas, group size is about 6 or 7 in the northeastern Atlantic and in the Mediterranean Sea. Although the dolphins are fairly common, they have not been studied much. In the 1980s, however,

two photo-identification surveys were begun off California and around the Azores Islands. Besides indicating local abundance, this research promises to reveal more about the social lives of Risso's dolphins.

Risso's dolphins are sometimes taken into captivity and kept with other closely related dolphins, such as the bottlenose. A number have mated across the species barrier. At one Japanese aquarium, 13 births occurred to mixed bottlenose and Risso's dolphin parents. Most offspring died at birth or shortly afterward, but one survived for more than six years, showing characteristics of both parents.

Grampus griseus
Size: 3.3 to 3.8 metres; 350 to 400 kilograms. Males slightly larger than females.
Calves at birth: 135 to 166 centimetres.
Teeth: 2 to 7 peglike teeth on each side of lower jaw only.
Food: Squid, octopuses and fish.
Habitat: Mainly deep offshore but also coastal waters.
Range: Tropical to temperate world ocean.
Status: Population unknown.

MELON-HEADED WHALE

Peponocephala electra
Size: 2.3 to 2.7 metres; 160 kilograms. Males slightly larger than females.
Calves at birth: 65 to 112 centimetres.
Teeth: 21 to 25 sharply pointed teeth on each side of upper and lower jaws.
Food: Squid and various small fish.
Habitat: Deep offshore waters.
Range: Tropical and subtropical world ocean.
Status: Population unknown.

Melon-headed whales travel close together in herds of 150 to 1,500 animals. They swim fast and barely break the water, whipping the sea surface into a froth. Despite ranging throughout the world ocean, melon-headed whales, like pygmy killer whales, are rarely reported at sea.

PYGMY KILLER WHALE

Feresa attenuata
Size: 2 to 2.9 metres; 150 to 170 kilograms. Males slightly larger than females.
Calves at birth: 53 to 82 centimetres.
Teeth: 11 to 13 teeth on each side of lower jaw; 8 to 11 smaller teeth in upper jaw.
Food: Probably fish. Also reported to attack dolphins.
Habitat: Deep offshore waters.
Range: Tropical and subtropical world ocean.
Status: Population unknown.

Until 1965, the only evidence of the pygmy killer whale – once called the rarest mammal on Earth – consisted of a couple of museum skulls. Then a Hawaii aquarium captured a live pygmy killer whale, and scientists finally examined the strange black animal with white lips.

The false killer whale, or pseudorca, as it is sometimes called, shares many attributes with orcas and pilot whales. Yet little is known about its life in the wild, partly because it is less common.

False killer whales live in tight pods that vary in size from fewer than 10 to more than 100 individuals. All ages and both sexes travel together. Jetting through the water with their black, torpedolike bodies, false killer whales can look menacing. Quick and agile, they execute high leaps and make rapid turns and sudden stops.

Much of this activity is associated with feeding. Although they eat primarily squid and large fish in deep offshore waters, false killer whales are opportunists and consume a wide variety of fish. Their adaptability is crucial, because in the tropical and warm temperate ocean where they live, food is not nearly as abundant as it is toward the poles. These dolphins have developed a bad reputation for stealing fish from fishermen's lines and have even been known to attack, and perhaps eat, dolphins escaping from tuna nets in the eastern tropical Pacific. There is one report of false killers attacking and killing a humpback whale calf in Hawaiian waters. Held responsible for depleting the fish populations around Japan, hundreds of false killer whales have been driven ashore there and slaughtered.

Pseudorca crassidens
Size: 4 to 5.5 metres; 1,200 to 2,000 kilograms. Males slightly larger than females.
Calves at birth: 157 to 183 centimetres.
Teeth: 8 to 11 large teeth on each side of upper and lower jaws.
Food: Squid and large fish such as tuna. Sometimes attacks dolphins escaping from tuna nets.
Habitat: Deep offshore waters.
Range: Tropical and warm temperate world ocean.
Status: Population unknown.

The big male arched his back and presented his giant dorsal fin at its full height – more than 1.5 metres. A nick at the top of the fin, a distinctive quarter-round chip, indicated that this was Top Notch, or A5. As the mature male's fin sliced the water, researchers also saw the scarred back of an older female named Scar, A9 – Top Notch's mother. For almost 20 years, the research team had been following Scar and Top Notch. Scar's female calves had gone on to have their own families, but the thirtyish Top Notch was still travelling with his mother, in the company of a third whale, a now mature male calf that Scar had given birth to in 1971 or 1972.

This account of Scar and her big boys is taken from field notes written a few months before Scar died in 1990, at about 58 years of age. The only thing that seems to alter such long-term associations is death. After their mother's death, Top Notch and his brother continued to travel together.

Since the early 1970s, researchers off Vancouver Island have followed and photographed orca families, or pods. With tens of thousands of photographs taken, it is the most intensive dolphin or porpoise study in the wild. Every orca in three communities along the British Columbia/Washington coast has been identified – some 330 individuals.

Two separate communities of resident whales can be seen in the area every month of the year – 250 whales in 19 pods. The northern community ranges from northern Vancouver Island to Alaska, while the southern community lives off southern Vancouver Island and in Puget Sound, Washington. The third community is made up of transient whales – about 80 whales in 30 pods.

Periodic visitors all along the British Columbia/Washington coast, the transient whales do not associate with the residents at all. With pointed dorsal fins, they also look slightly different from the other orcas, and they travel in smaller groups of only 2 to 7 individuals per pod, while resident pods have 5 to 50 individuals. Their diet is also distinctive. Transients eat mainly marine mammals, including seals, sea lions and, occasionally, dolphins and whales. Residents eat fish such as salmon.

The photo-identification method has been the lifework of the late Michael Bigg and his associates, Graeme Ellis, Ian MacAskie, John Ford and Ken Balcomb, although many others have contributed to the study. The photographs are the key, serving as "fingerprints" that researchers can use to identify each individual and to determine which orca travels with which other individuals. Thousands of photographs showing two or more orcas close to each other have verified field sightings.

Analyzing such associations, some two dozen researchers engaged in the

Orcinus orca
Size: Males 6.7 to 7 metres (maximum 9.8 metres); 4,000 to 5,000 kilograms. Females 5.5 to 6.5 metres (maximum 7 metres); 2,500 to 3,000 kilograms.
Calves at birth: 208 to 276 centimetres.
Teeth: 10 to 12 conical teeth on each side of upper and lower jaws.
Food: Fish (salmon, cod, herring and others), seals, sea lions, squid, sea turtles and sometimes other dolphins and whales.
Habitat: Coastal and offshore waters.
Range: World ocean.
Status: Population unknown, but probably at least in the tens of thousands.

study have determined that the social order of the resident orcas apparently revolves around the female adults. The smallest resident whale unit is a maternal group that is composed of a mother and her offspring. Male offspring stay with their mothers. Only females leave the maternal group to form their own maternal groups, although they probably stay in the same subpod with their mother and other sisters or cousins. When the subpod reaches a certain size, it may form a new pod around the dominant female.

Another way to investigate the relationships among orca pods in a community is to listen to them. Orca dialects were discovered by John Ford in the late 1970s. Working off Vancouver Island, Ford discovered that no two orca pods sound exactly alike. Every pod has some unique sounds. Within each community are "clans" – groups of pods that share certain sounds. Ford says that because the sounds of each pod are probably learned from the mother, the number of shared sounds between pods likely reveals how closely related the pods are.

Ford came to the conclusion that pods with dialects 90 percent the same probably had a recent common ancestor. Pods with only 25 to 50 percent similarity are more distantly related. The three clans in the northern community and the one clan in the southern community have no sounds in common; they actually sound as different as orcas from Iceland and Antarctica. Dialects used by animals living in the same region are unique to orcas. Humans are the only other species with true dialects.

Orcas, *left*, rest in Johnstone Strait off northern Vancouver Island, British Columbia. During these quiet periods, orcas float at the surface, breathing slowly several times over a minute or two, then submerge for three or four minutes before resurfacing in almost the same spot and repeating the pattern. Orcas do not have regular daily resting times and may sleep for only 10 to 20 minutes; the longest sleep period observed in the orcas off Vancouver Island was four hours.

LONG-FINNED PILOT WHALE

Long-finned pilot whales seem to prefer squid. So accomplished are they at tracking squid that other dolphins, birds and even fishermen will let the whales "pilot" them to squid as well as to the herring, mackerel and capelin the squid feed on. But in some places, pilot whales themselves are the object of the hunt.

Via television and news photographs, millions of people have seen herds of long-finned pilot whales lying in pools of blood along the coast of the Faroe Islands, north of Scotland. Every year, the Islanders drive the whales to shore and slaughter entire herds. It is easy to do once the whales are located. Pilot whales are so social that if one strands, even accidentally, the others usually come ashore too. If individuals are pushed or towed out to sea, they often return — only to die.

Pilot whale, or "pothead," hunts have taken place in several areas of the world during the past century, including off the coast of Newfoundland. The Faroe Islanders have been hunting pilot whales for at least four centuries and perhaps thousands of years. But today's Islanders no longer depend on whales for food. Population studies have been conducted but are not complete. Still, the traditional hunt, which harvests about 2,000 animals a year, carries on.

Globicephala melas
Size: Males 5.5 to 6.2 metres (maximum 8.5 metres); 3,000 to 3,500 kilograms. Females 3.8 to 5.4 metres (maximum 6 metres); 1,800 to 2,500 kilograms.
Calves at birth: 177 centimetres.
Teeth: 8 to 12 peglike teeth on each side of upper and lower jaws.
Food: Squid, octopuses and fish (cod, mackerel, hake and others).
Habitat: Mainly deep offshore waters.
Range: Temperate and subpolar Atlantic, Indian and South Pacific.
Status: Population unknown. Has been caught by shore-based whalers, especially in the North Atlantic.

Most scientific work on pilot whales has been done with the long-finned pilot whale in the cold North Atlantic. The closely related short-finned pilot whale lives in warmer waters. From 1988 to 1991, Jim and Sara Heimlich-Boran studied groups of short-finned pilot whales off Tenerife, in the Canary Islands, photographing their dorsal fins to identify them.

The Heimlich-Borans usually found pilot whales moving through areas with a water depth of about 1,000 metres. The whales seemed to feed mainly at night, when squid come up from the depths. Typical group size is 10 to 30, although a few pods are as large as 60. Some individuals stay to-gether in core groups of five or six; others move between groups and subgroups. Like orcas, pilot whales live long lives – up to 65 years for females. In all, the researchers have identified 445 individuals off the Canary Islands. About half have been observed two or more times.

The calm water of the study area provided an ideal resting place. During rest periods, the pilot whales travelled short distances and hovered at the surface. From time to time, bottlenose dolphins would arrive, and the whales became more active. Then they played, surfing on ocean swells – an amusing sight as the bulbous heads rode on the waves.

Globicephala macrorhynchus
Size: Males 4.5 to 5 metres (maximum 5.5 metres); 2,500 kilograms. Females 3.3 to 3.6 metres (maximum 5 metres); 1,300 kilograms.
Calves at birth: 140 centimetres.
Teeth: 7 to 9 peglike teeth on each side of upper and lower jaws.
Food: Squid and various fish.
Habitat: Mainly deep offshore waters.
Range: Tropical and warm temperate world ocean.
Status: Population unknown, but common within its range.

Dolphins and porpoises are hunters, feeding mainly on various species of fish. Many hunt in groups and search for large schools of prey, depending on what is available. Each fish species has its own annual cycle of movements, and dolphins and porpoises often follow fish schools or seem to know where to intercept them – perhaps by "tasting" chemicals from the fish, such as urine and feces.

Some dolphins, however, prefer squid. The squid-eaters are pilot whales, false killer whales, melon-headed whales and Risso's dolphins, but other dolphins sometimes take squid as well.

Some dolphins have part-time preferences. Rough-toothed dolphins eat mollusks, and tucuxi eat shrimp. One river dolphin, the boto, eats "armoured" varieties of freshwater bottom fish, crushing them with its flat, molarlike teeth.

Orcas, the largest dolphins, eat almost all of the above and individ-ually consume more than any other dolphin. One mature captive male devoured up to 160 kilograms of fish a day, but the average is 79 kilograms for males, 63 kilograms for females and 16 kilograms for babies when they stop nursing. In captivity, orcas eat dead fish, mostly herring, although some marine parks give them salmon or other fish species. In the wild, orcas catch dozens of species of fish and squid. Many orcas specialize in taking marine mammals – seals, sea lions, other dolphins, porpoises and sometimes even large whales.

Scientists determine the diet of dolphins and porpoises mainly by examining the stomachs of animals that strand on beaches and die or are found floating dead at sea or washed ashore. Occasionally, they find and analyze feces. Only rarely does a scientist actually see, much less photograph, a dolphin in the act of catching a fish. Feeding usually occurs un-derwater, obscured from view. Even at the surface, it happens quickly. However, when researchers in British Columbia suspect that orcas are feeding on salmon, they scoop nets into the water to recover the shimmering fish scales which often fall off and float at the surface; each species of salmon has different scales. Pilot whales often follow squid, which is good evidence of a food preference. The movements of other dolphins also sometimes correspond with those of squid or fish.

Probably all species of dolphins and porpoises use their sonar to "see" fish prey. But when orcas hunt seals or other marine mammals that have better hearing than fish, they keep quiet, watch their prey and sneak up on it. Of course, river dolphins, most of which have limited vision in muddy rivers, have to rely on sonar. When the prey is located, it is quickly snatched or chased and trapped against the river bottom or an underwater rock wall. In the open sea, schools of fish are sometimes corralled by a large herd of dolphins and forced to the water's surface, which acts as a wall. Researchers and fishermen often see fish jumping furiously out of the water in a desperate attempt to escape.

Dolphins and porpoises use their teeth to grasp prey. An orca may bite a sea lion into pieces, and the boto crushes its armoured food. But dolphins and porpoises do not chew as they eat – fish, squid and pieces of larger prey are swallowed whole.

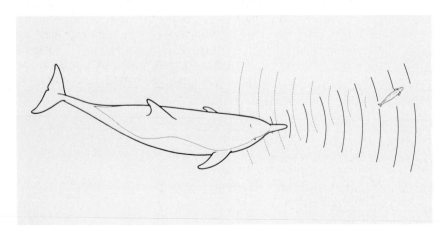

Dolphin sonar, or echolocation, *far left*, enables dolphins to find and identify their food, then capture it. High-pitched clicks sent out in a steady stream intercept objects in the dolphin's path. By listening to the echoes reflected off the fish's body, the dolphin obtains a "sound picture" that allows it to hunt in deep, dark waters or during the night. Although the U.S. Navy has studied the sonar abilities of bottlenose dolphins for several decades, the sonar it has developed remains a crude imitation of dolphin sonar. In this sequence of photographs, *left*, taken at Punta Norte, in southern Argentina, an orca charges a seal, almost beaching itself in the process. Note the sharp, curved teeth used to grasp the seal. The orca may toss the animal around to stun or kill it before swallowing it whole. Although most dolphins, including orcas, eat fish, certain orca populations specialize in seals, sea lions and even whales. When orcas hunt larger prey, they usually remain silent and do not use echolocation. Marine mammals have such good hearing that orcas must sneak up on seals and sea lions to catch them.

Dolphins and porpoises are social mammals, even more so than most species of large whales. Many live as part of a group, side by side with others to which they are more or less related. They probably use some of their sounds to communicate with each other. The group dynamic is the key to understanding much of their behaviour and is certainly crucial to their success as species.

Yet the size of the group and the type and strength of the social bonds, as well as location and behaviour,

vary considerably by species. In general, the largest groups are among the oceanic dolphins, such as spotted and common dolphins, which gather in groups of up to 500 in the eastern tropical Pacific. Melon-headed whales often associate in groups of 150 to 1,500, and striped dolphins sometimes travel in groups of 3,000. But typical numbers in most parts of the world, even of these species, are in the dozens. Many of these herds contain both sexes and all ages, but some species are further divided into

adults of both sexes; females and calves; and immature animals of both sexes. Sometimes, male adults swim alone or in a separate group.

River dolphins and porpoises form the smallest groups. Often solitary, river dolphins rarely gather in herds of more than 10 to 15 individuals. And most true porpoises are found in groups of fewer than 10. Dall's porpoises, however, sometimes travel in schools of up to 3,000.

Dolphins hunt in large numbers because it gives them an advantage in cornering or corralling schools of fish. Sometimes, several species of dolphins hunt side by side, but it is difficult to determine whether they are feeding separately or actually co-ordinating hunting manoeuvres. Obviously, the more dolphins there are in a group, the more fish they will need to catch in order to make the reward worth sharing.

Some species have complex associations. An individual orca, for example, might belong to many different groups at the same time. The resident orcas of British Columbia and Washington State are born into a *maternal group*, made up of brothers and sisters of all ages led by their mothers. One or more maternal groups make up a *subpod*. In subpods, the breeding females are usually sisters and the youngsters are siblings or first cousins. Subpods may travel independently for days or even months, but generally, they travel with other subpods as a *pod*.

Each pod has its own dialect, with

some sounds unique to the pod. Pods that share some sounds are called *clans*. There are four resident clans off British Columbia and Washington State, three that make up the northern community and one the southern community. A *community* is composed of pods that associate from time to time, often for parts of every day during the summer. Two or more pods from a community travel together as a *superpod*.

Is an orca community equivalent to a *population*, or breeding unit? Because orca communities do not mix, they would each appear to represent a population. However, recent genetic studies have revealed that the northern and southern communities were probably once a single community and still form only one population.

Scientists can count herds and observe obvious behaviour, such as different methods of hunting. But there are other ways they learn about the intimate details of social behaviour. In the past, scientists often killed animals to study them, and many valuable things were learned this way. For the most part, though, it is no longer acceptable to kill wild animals to study them. Yet all species suffer natural and, from time to time, accidental deaths, and it is important that scientists use such opportunities to learn what they can.

When an entire group strands and dies on a beach, for instance, it is then possible to establish the sexes and ages in the group. Through dissections, biologists can assess the fitness

of the animals and perhaps discover what killed them. The number of times each female has ovulated can be determined by studying the reproductive organs. Layers in the teeth of some species can be counted to calculate the age.

Many things, however, can be learned only by patiently watching and monitoring the behaviour and movement of live animals. The revolution in such study began in the 1970s, thanks to new photographic techniques, in particular, and to radio-tagging and satellite-monitoring technology. Individual animals and groups can now be followed from birth to death. The full results of this work are very slow in coming, but the rewards are great and are responsible for much of the excitement in dolphin and whale research today.

Spinner dolphins rest near the top of the water column, *left*, while common dolphins, *above*, race along the water's surface. As with all mammals, the social lives of dolphins start with the bond between mothers and calves. Dolphin group size varies with species, region and behaviour. Spinner and common dolphins sometimes travel in hunting herds of several thousand in the tropical Pacific, where schools of fish are large enough to make it worthwhile. In other areas of the world, where fish are found in lower concentrations, the herds may number only 5 to 10 individuals.

The intimate details of dolphin courtship, mating and birth – the reproductive cycle – have remained largely hidden from view. Many researchers who have spent 5 to 10 seasons in the field still have only a vague idea of dolphin reproductive habits. Most have never witnessed a mating or a birth in the wild. With persistence and luck, however, a few researchers have learned something about these events.

Unlike the large whales, dolphins and porpoises appear to have no special mating and calving grounds to which they travel in winter. Researchers have noticed that with some species, such as orcas and bottlenose dolphins, new calves appear at certain times of the year. This suggests that mating is somewhat seasonal. By monitoring captive dolphins, scientists have determined the exact length of pregnancy (gestation period) in some species. For bottlenose dolphins, it is 12 months; for orcas, 17½ months. But the gestation period is unknown for most dolphin species.

Are dolphins and porpoises monogamous (mating with a single individual for life) or promiscuous (mating with many others)? Scientists have strong evidence that most dolphins are promiscuous. Only river dolphins and some porpoise species stay in small enough groups that they might be monogamous. But small groups alone, of course, do not tell the whole story, since the groups may change over time. The key to learning more about reproductive habits, as with other social behaviour, is the identification and sexing of individuals and long-term monitoring.

For years, scientists have suspected that some of the interactions they see routinely are probably courtship, or preludes to mating behaviour. Recent research on bottlenose dolphins has provided the first detailed insights. The breakthrough came in Shark Bay at Monkey Mia, Australia, where researchers have been able to witness dolphin behaviour under ideal field conditions. The bottlenose dolphins there associate close to shore in fairly calm water and are particularly accessible to human visitors in a small boat. Some 300 dolphins – each named by researchers – have been closely watched for two decades, first by Elizabeth Gawain and, for the past 10 years, by Rachel Smolker, Richard Conner and Andrew Richards. In recent years, the researchers have focused on the exuberant young males, whose behaviour had been called

"playful" by most observers. What were the dolphins really doing?

As adolescents, most male bottlenose dolphins form tight, long-term bonds with one or two other males. These buddies swim, bow-ride, fish and play together. From time to time, they will herd a female, trying to get her to travel with them; eventually, they attempt to mate with her.

When there are few potential mates, however, male competition can become fierce. Two groups of buddies gang up and sometimes steal a female away from another group. Only one group of buddies stays with the female, the role of the others having been simply to help out. But days later, the favour may be forgotten, and the gang that helped may join up with a third group of buddies to steal the female again.

Females, the researchers found, are more varied in their associations. Some stay alone, some travel with a few other females, and some move from subgroup to subgroup. Off Florida, where the females have been studied extensively, they stayed with other related females but sometimes went visiting.

Dolphins and porpoises mate belly to belly, like whales. Most females do not conceive every year. Bottlenose dolphins give birth to calves every four to five years on average, as do orcas. The babies are usually born tail first. An assisting female may help the calf to the surface for its first breath of air. In some species, such as orcas, this job may be performed by

a male – or the calf will surface by itself. After mating, dolphin and porpoise fathers do not appear to take an active role in caring for their offspring. But several species, such as pilot whales, Atlantic spotted dolphins and bottlenose dolphins, have other females that act as babysitters.

Bottlenose dolphin calves nurse for 18 to 20 months but may remain under their mother's care and tutelage for three to six years. A few other dolphin species stay with their mothers to the age of maturity and longer. A young female orca leaves her mother's side only when her first calf is born, at about age 15. Even then, she will probably remain in her mother's subgroup for life. Like few other animals, orcas share with their close relatives the key events of their lives – from birth to death.

Spinner dolphins, *far left*, mate in the tropical Atlantic off northern Brazil. All dolphins and porpoises mate belly to belly. Orcas, *left*, cavort in a prelude to mating. The penis appears only when erect, protruding from the genital region. A mother spinner and her two calves, *above*, one a newborn, swim near the surface. Even after a year or two of nursing, calves may remain with their mothers. In some dolphin species, the older calf leaves when the newborn arrives. Others, such as the spinner, linger for several years. With orcas, female calves stay for about a decade, until they themselves give birth to their first calf. Even then, they continue to travel nearby in the mother's expanding subpod—probably for life.

DOLPHINS AND HUMANS

People have identified with dolphins for thousands of years. Several early accounts from the Mediterranean area tell of children riding on dolphins. According to the Roman scholar Pliny the Elder, a boy from Lake Lucrino, near Naples, made friends with a dolphin that carried him across the water to school every day. Another boy, from Hippo (now part of Tunisia), became friends with a dolphin after the dolphin saved him from drowning. These stories, thought to be true, were written almost 2,000 years ago, in the first century A.D.

Christina Lockyer of the Sea Mammal Research Unit in England investigated these as well as modern-day cases of "friendly," sociable dolphins. She took to the water and swam with dolphins – and went for many rides herself. She was able to confirm various reports of encounters between friendly dolphins and humans:

☐ In the mid-1950s, in New Zealand, a young female bottlenose dolphin became friendly with swimmers, both children and adults. Opo, as she was called, allowed people to sit on her back while she moved slowly through the water.

☐ In the 1960s, in Monkey Mia, Australia, a woman began feeding and touching a group of bottlenose dolphins that regularly came into the shallows, in water less than one metre deep. From 1966 to 1972, a dolphin known as Old Charlie became so familiar, he permitted children to sit on

his back. Today, 100,000 people a year come to wade into the water to meet and touch the dolphins. People offer them dead fish, which the dolphins either eat, play with or ignore. Only some of the dolphins swim in – seven regulars, by the most recent count. The others remain out in the bay.

☐ In the 1960s, a female bottlenose dolphin befriended a family in Florida. After two months, Georgy Girl seemed to be encouraging the family to touch her and began carrying people on her back after swimming between their legs.

☐ In 1981, an older 4.1-metre male bottlenose dolphin named Percy began following a fishing boat on its daily run off Cornwall, England. After almost two years, he allowed people to touch him, hang on to his dorsal fin and go for rides. But then he became unpredictable. Sometimes, he was gentle, but at other times, he would butt swimmers in the chest, smash surfboards and carry people out to sea. It was a reminder that wild animals should be approached with caution. Since then, some scientists have begun to question the wisdom of taming or making friends with wild dolphins.

Which dolphin species are "sociable"? Most are bottlenose dolphins, although orcas, Risso's dolphins and others have also participated in such encounters. The gregarious dolphins tend to be either old or young animals. In each case, the dolphins have revealed individual personalities. Many have been solitary creatures,

but exceptions include the regulars at Monkey Mia. Perhaps there are various reasons for accepting humans as temporary social companions. All seem to have had a history of persistent taming by one or more people over a period of months or years. Only a few of the dozens of cases – notably Percy and another dolphin, called Donald – became aggressive to the point of being dangerous to humans. Both were older male bottlenose dolphins whose activities off Britain's coast were closely monitored by Lockyer and others.

The best explanation for such behaviour might simply be that bottlenose dolphins, as well as other dolphins, are intensely curious. Such curiosity is a necessary part of being an opportunistic predator. It can be crucial to the dolphin's survival to check out new additions to its environment. In every case reported here, a curious and close approach to a human was repeatedly encouraged, and the dolphin responded. In time, the animals grew used to human company. What seemed to be play behaviour was the result. The dolphins may somehow have been trying to incorporate people into their group.

Some scientists have worked with these tamed dolphins, engaging them as partners in their research, testing their audio and diving abilities and swimming speeds. Eventually, however, the dolphins disappear, leaving the researchers to ponder the mysteries of sociable dolphins – why they come and why they go.

In some parts of the world, dolphins regularly swim into shallow water and accept—or play with—dead fish offered by humans. These bottlenose dolphins, *left*, live off the coast of Honduras, in the Caribbean Sea. *Above:* Atlantic spotted dolphins in the Bahamas will approach boats and people in the water. Since the early 1980s, people on guided trips have been able to swim with these wild dolphins. Because the dolphins are so accessible, they have provided researchers with an ideal opportunity to study their underwater behaviour. The researchers are able to see the dolphins' whole bodies and so can determine the sex of the animals as well as whether the females are pregnant.

Like whale watching, observing wild dolphins and porpoises is becoming a more and more popular pastime. Anyone who lives near the ocean or takes seaside holidays can see them. The secret is to become a student of dolphin habits and find out which species can be seen precisely where and at what time of year. A good naturalist guide or a guidebook can also help. Whether observing from shore or from a boat, you will find that binoculars, a camera with a long lens, warm clothes, sunscreen and a thermos with a hot drink are all helpful.

Watching from shore is the simplest and least expensive method, but it may require more patience. For good visibility, choose a day when the ocean is calm and there is little or no fog. Throughout the northern hemisphere, the two aquatic mammals that are most commonly sighted close to shore are bottlenose dolphins and harbour porpoises. Despite their name, harbour porpoises have mostly abandoned harbours and other urban or industrial areas as habitats, perhaps because of excess traffic and the scarcity of fish in these polluted areas. Try to select sections of coastline with clean water – especially places that are known for good fishing. A high headland or pier is ideal.

Some promising regions from which to observe harbour porpoises, especially in summer, include:
☐ New Brunswick and Maine on the Bay of Fundy
☐ Québec in the lower river and the Gulf of St. Lawrence
☐ the coast from central California to British Columbia

The best regions for summer sightings of bottlenose dolphins are:
☐ southern Virginia and North Carolina, from Cape Hatteras to Cape Lookout
☐ along the Atlantic and Gulf coasts of Florida
☐ the Moray Firth of Scotland
☐ southern California

Other dolphins that swim close to shore include orcas (off British Columbia and Washington State), spinner and spotted dolphins (around the Hawaiian Islands), Atlantic whitesided dolphins (near Cape Cod, Massachusetts) and Dall's porpoises (from

British Columbia to southeast Alaska).

Many dolphin and porpoise species, however, remain offshore most or all of the year. A guided boat tour can escort you to areas where dolphins are known to feed or socialize. Tours may be offered as part of seabird- or whale-watching trips, but dolphins and porpoises are the cetaceans most likely to be seen. Contact provincial, state or national tourist boards, or check nature magazines for up-to-date listings of such tours.

An experienced naturalist guide with a specialist tour company not only knows where to go but can also provide background and insights into dolphin behaviour. For the inexperienced observer, it can be difficult to interpret fleeting glimpses of dolphins at the surface. Since dolphins spend 95 percent of their time underwater, some guides carry portable listening systems to keep track of them and to tune in to their underwater sounds.

Dolphins and porpoises can also be seen in aquariums and marine parks. The first bottlenose dolphins were captured and exhibited during the 1860s, but success in keeping them was limited until the 1950s. Since then, attempts have been made to keep members of half of all dolphin and porpoise species in captivity. Bottlenose dolphins are the most commonly shown, with almost 3,000 captured to date for display in aquariums. More than any other dolphin or porpoise, bottlenose dolphins have bred successfully in captivity. They are second in popularity only to orcas, which draw millions of people every year to 17 parks in Canada, the United States, Japan, Hong Kong, Latin America and Europe.

Whether or not it is right for humans to put dolphins on display and to train them to perform has become a controversial issue in recent years. Performing dolphins have entertained millions of people and have introduced them to a fascinating mammal of the sea. In fact, the only close-up experience most people have with a dolphin is at an aquarium. Directors and owners of aquariums call captives "ambassadors for their species" and argue that people will not be interested in saving something they do not know.

But what do we really learn from captive dolphins? Dolphins are trained to perform the same acts over and over again. In captivity, they can no longer hunt; instead, they circle and pace a small, bare pool several times their length, a tiny fraction of their range in the wild. Their social life is severely limited compared with the large families of the wild. The quality of food and the standards of medical care are high at the best marine parks and aquariums, yet certain animals simply cannot adjust to such restricted conditions and suffer excessive stress, sometimes dying prematurely.

Some valuable scientific studies have been conducted on captive dolphins and porpoises, but they have been undertaken primarily at the few institutions that emphasize research.

Knowledge gained by studying dolphins in captivity may one day help save those in the wild. But if science is the purpose of keeping them captive, far fewer dolphins need to be captured. In fact, performing dolphins have been mainly a money-making attraction.

Rather than capturing dolphins, some people say, we should get to know them through quality films and books. If we want to see the animals firsthand, we can go on dolphin- and whale-watching tours and observe them from land-based lookouts.

Should dolphins and porpoises be regarded as "resources" to be used for our entertainment, education and scientific knowledge? Or should they be left alone—mostly or even completely—to live their lives in the wild? What do you think?

A Dall's porpoise in the North Pacific, *left*, is one of several species, including orcas, Pacific white-sided dolphins and harbour porpoises, that can be seen on increasingly popular dolphin- and porpoise-watching tours. Until recently, most dolphin and porpoise watching took place in conjunction with whale-watching tours, but people are becoming interested in these mammals on their own. *Above:* Many people are introduced to dolphins at a marine park or aquarium. These bottlenose dolphins at Marine World Africa U.S.A. in California perform regular shows that are partly natural behaviours and partly circus routines.

How close have humans and dolphins come to communicating with one another? Scientists such as John C. Lilly, working with captive bottlenose dolphins in the early 1960s, thought it would be only a few years before there was a communication breakthrough. Impressed with their large brains, Lilly performed many audio experiments attempting to show that dolphins were communicating with each other. In an effort to facilitate communication, he began to use computers to translate human words into dolphin whistles and to send messages. Much of his experimental work has never been published.

In one well-known Lilly experiment, a woman lived in a pool with a bottlenose dolphin named Peter as her only companion for several months. Sleeping in an often damp bed above the pool, she was ever on call. Peter was a boisterous, demanding roommate, and the woman soon realized that he wanted to interact much more than she did. While a basic communication did develop, similar to that between a dog and a human, deeper exchanges—of dolphin whistles or human words—proved impossible.

Lilly's work ended in the 1980s. Since then, researchers led by Louis M. Herman have developed a new approach to communication studies with captive bottlenose dolphins at the University of Hawaii. Their goals have been to discover how dolphins process information, both through sight and sound, how they learn and how they communicate. Herman's

research has verified earlier findings that dolphins have good memories and can mimic a wide variety of sounds. Able to store new information, they can also update old information rapidly.

In one experiment, Herman played up to eight different short sounds on an underwater speaker in the dolphin's tank. Then another sound was played, sometimes one of the previous eight, sometimes an entirely new sound. The dolphin had to decide whether it had heard the sound before. About 70 percent of the time, the dolphin responded correctly. If the list was shortened, however, to one or two sounds, the results were 90 per-

cent correct. Like humans given such tests, the dolphins found the recent items easiest to remember.

The dolphin's most impressive accomplishment is its ability to understand sentences expressed in either an artificial acoustic or a visual language. In the experiments, the "words" of the language are sounds generated by a computer and broadcast via an underwater speaker. First the dolphin learns words such as fetch, ball and hoop. The words refer to (1) objects in the tank; (2) actions that might be taken in connection with the objects; and (3) modifiers of place or location. In "sentences" of two or more words, the dolphin is then told to do something. The level of understanding is measured by the accuracy and reliability with which the dolphin carries out the instructions.

Dolphins perform very well on such tests. To more than 600 two-word-sentence instructions, the dolphins gave correct responses about 80 percent of the time. They also understood "new" instructions almost as well as familiar ones, with only a slight advantage to the familiar. New instructions consisted of fresh combinations of words that either obeyed the language rules or, in a few cases, were logical extensions of existing rules.

Gradually, the dolphins seemed to master sentence form and use. They were taught to respond to sentences up to five words long. Then visual symbols or gestures, as well as auditory signals, were tried. Comprehension for a dolphin trained with visuals was the same as that for a dolphin trained with sound.

These and other experiments show that dolphins can learn rules and understand certain abstract concepts. And they can work with both auditory and visual symbols. Compared with apes taught to use American sign language – an exclusively visual medium for communication – the dolphins have more range. The apes, on the other hand, learn more quickly in tests involving symbols. Of course, all of these are laboratory feats and prove nothing about life in the wild – for dolphins or apes.

Herman and other researchers, however, believe the society of the

wild bottlenose dolphin is a socially dependent world in which learning everything about the other members of a group may be crucial for survival. Within these dolphin societies, says Herman, social rules or conventions that may be complex might govern social relationships, social roles and social behaviours.

In the future, trained dolphins may be able to grasp more complex human-taught vocabularies. But this does not necessarily mean that dolphins have their own language. We cannot know where research will lead. Many scientists feel that we can only glimpse what really goes on inside the mind of a wild dolphin.

Pacific white-sided dolphins, *far left*, perform for their trainer as part of a Sea World show in San Diego, California. The slick choreography is accomplished through hand and audio signals that cue the dolphins to begin a "behaviour" and signal a reward once it has been completed. Handlers develop a basic communication with the animals by using a food-reward system. While the level of communication is similar to what you might have with the family dog, work with captive dolphins at the University of Hawaii has revealed that the communication can go much further. Here, bottlenose dolphins have learned to recognize a modest vocabulary of words— subjects, verbs and objects—as represented by visual and audio signals. They respond to and comprehend unfamiliar "sentences" almost as well as familiar ones. The effort to understand dolphin communication and to teach dolphins a symbolic language continues. In an attempt to interpret dolphin sounds, some scientists make sonograms, or visual printouts. The signature whistle of an Atlantic spotted dolphin, *left*, shows the frequency, or pitch, of the sound. Like bottlenose and other dolphins, spotted dolphins have whistles that are unique to each individual. Since sounds can carry for many kilometres, this may be how dolphins recognize one another even at great distances.

Our knowledge about the health of living dolphin and porpoise populations is sadly incomplete. Only five species have been determined to be "vulnerable" or "endangered," and most others are described as "insufficiently known." Too many times, we can say only that the "total population is unknown" or the "number killed is unknown" or "much more research is necessary." The grave danger is that some unique and fascinating dolphin species will be gone before detailed research and population censuses can be carried out.

Urgent action is needed to avert the deaths of hundreds of thousands of dolphins and porpoises that are accidentally killed every year. Some years, the figure has surpassed half a million worldwide – all because of human activities. This is more than 10 times the number of large whales that were slaughtered in the early 1930s, the worst years of whaling.

Dolphins may be dying because of pollution from dumping at sea, oil spills and farm pesticides and other chemical runoff that enter the rivers, then flow to the sea. In recent years, particularly in the Mediterranean and off the east coast of the United States, dolphins have been dying by the hundreds, then washing ashore, victims of unexplained viruses or weakened immune systems that may have been caused by pollution. In some cases, food poisoning from red-tide organisms may have been the cause. But some scientists believe that pollution from PCBs, DDT and other contami-

nants is responsible. The contaminants are picked up in plankton, then they move to fish and other plankton-eaters and, finally, to dolphins and porpoises. The contaminants might not cause immediate death but, rather, a weakening of the immune system that leaves the animals more susceptible to disease.

Dolphins and porpoises are commonly killed in encounters with fishermen in every ocean. Before the 1970s, fishermen in the North Pacific off British Columbia and Washington State and in the North Atlantic off Iceland shot orcas that they believed were scaring away or taking "their" fish. Fishermen in Japan and other

places, angry that dolphins "steal" fish off their hooks or frighten fish away, drive great herds of dolphins into the shallows, killing them. Bottlenose dolphins, false killer whales, Risso's dolphins and Pacific white-sided dolphins are among the victims. Fishermen either sell them for meat and fertilizer or leave them to rot.

Some individual dolphins do learn to follow fishermen for a "free" lunch, yet such behaviour is uncommon, and it certainly does not threaten fish species. No dolphin or porpoise, no sea mammal, can compete with modern fishing fleets.

The biggest threat to dolphins is the fisherman's net. Nets sometimes kill

dolphins accidentally, while other times, fishermen "set" on dolphins. In the eastern tropical Pacific and in other seas, tuna fishermen follow dolphins to locate schools of tuna. These fishermen are mainly on the lookout for spotted dolphins, but they also watch for the spinner, common and Fraser's dolphins that live in this part of the open Pacific and often associate with yellowfin tuna. The fishermen set their purse seines around the herd of dolphins, catching the dolphins and, down below, the commercially valuable tuna.

In the 1960s and early 1970s, between 200,000 and 500,000 dolphins a year became entangled and suffocated in tuna nets. It was a staggering number and one that resulted in the Marine Mammal Protection Act, which was passed in the United States in 1972 to protect dolphins. Some nets were redesigned with escape panels so that dolphins could swim free. But most of the tuna boats were sold to other countries, which simply passed along the problem.

By the early 1980s, an estimated 80 percent of the spinner dolphins in the eastern Pacific had been killed. Environmental groups in Canada, the United States and Britain asked people to support dolphins by refusing to eat tuna. This consumer boycott helped create "dolphin-safe tuna"— the marketing of tuna that have been caught on lines or by methods which ensure that no dolphins are killed. By the early 1990s, dolphin kills by U.S. fishermen were down to fewer than

10,000 per year, and most U.S. fishermen had moved away from the eastern tropical Pacific. But fishermen from other countries continue to use dolphins to catch tuna in the eastern tropical Pacific and, to an unknown extent, in other areas of the world ocean as well.

Besides dying in tuna nets, dolphins are killed in every part of the world ocean by gill nets, trawls and even long-line fishing. The most indiscriminate killers – the new ocean drift nets – are up to 50 kilometres long. Made of strong nylon monofilament that dolphins cannot always detect, these nets are called "walls of death" by environmentalists. Tens of thousands of dolphins and porpoises are caught in drift nets every year, as are many noncommercial species of fish, birds, turtles and other marine mammals. Most of these go to waste, however, when drift-net fishermen haul in their nets, keeping the tuna and discarding the rest.

Some countries have banned these nets within their own territorial waters, up to 325 kilometres offshore. It's a start, but nets still crisscross the open seas, where neither government nor reason rules. In 1991, however, the United Nations General Assembly called for a global moratorium on long high-seas drift nets. UN resolutions are not binding, but Japan, Taiwan and South Korea – the three main drift-netting countries – agreed to reduce their operations immediately and to stop them completely by the end of 1993.

The activities of humans and dolphins are increasingly coming into conflict. Bottlenose dolphins, *left*, hunt for food at sunrise side by side with shrimp trawlers in the Gulf of Mexico. In general, fishing nets are the biggest dolphin killers, but widespread ocean pollution is a future threat. This bottlenose dolphin, *above*, stranded on a New Jersey beach in 1987, where rescuers battled unsuccessfully to save its life. Over an eight-month period in 1987 and 1988, 750 bottlenose dolphins stranded and died from New Jersey to Florida— about half of the coastal population. Food poisoning from red-tide organisms was probably a factor in the deaths, but pollution from PCBs, DDT and other contaminants was thought to be partly to blame.

It is not enough for humans to stop killing dolphins and porpoises for food or other resources. We must reserve a place for them in the sea. They need habitat, as do all animals – places free from fishing nets, oil spills, pollution and too much ship traffic. We must also consider all the species in the dolphins' food chain. Which fish are the dolphins eating? Which fish and other organisms are the fish eating? To protect habitats, all these things must be taken into account.

The habitat needs of dolphins and porpoises vary by species and by population. To establish real needs, we must map their movements and understand their basic biology and social behaviour. Where do they travel? Is it mostly to the same places and along the same routes from year to year? Where do they give birth? Where do they socialize, rest and play? Do these activities require protected habitats?

In general, the closer dolphins live to shore and to people, the more problems they face. Many harbour porpoises and bottlenose dolphins raise their young and eat fish near shore. They are much more affected by ship traffic and pollution – runoff from agricultural land and dump sites – than are the dolphin herds that live and feed in the deep waters off the continental shelf. Atlantic humpbacked and other tropical coastal dolphins are losing their food supplies with the cutting of the mangroves that serve as fish nurseries.

The greatest impact on dolphin habitat has been felt by the river

dolphins and vaquitas, found in the Gulf of California, Mexico. These are the most threatened of all whales and dolphins. In China, baijis have been killed by fishing hooks, and only about 300 remain. The bhulan, with fewer than 500 left, is now restricted to limited areas between irrigation barrages in the Indus River system of Pakistan, where some illegal hunting persists. And on the Amazon River, dams, industrial developments and extensive logging are reducing dolphin habitat.

For orcas off the west coast of Canada, some of the key habitat questions have been answered. After more than two decades of studying orca behaviour, we know that they return to the same waters year after year and that they prefer certain places to others. A favourite

area is around Robson Bight, off northern Vancouver Island. Here, in the clean water near the estuary and along the shore, orcas spend a few minutes to a few hours most summer days resting, playing and rubbing on the special smooth-pebble beaches that are found only here. They also feed on salmon that school along the shore before spawning.

In 1982, Robson Bight became a marine ecological reserve – the first orca sanctuary in the world. Public protest halted the creation of a log port that had been planned for Robson Bight. But the whales needed some land protection as well, and 505 hectares – including 10.7 kilometres of shoreline – were set aside in the late 1980s. Still, logging activities in the Tsitika River Valley at Robson Bight have pushed the clear-cuts to within four kilometres of open water. The wilderness character of the area is quickly disappearing. The water quality of the river may change, and the salmon runs could be harmed.

In order to save dolphins and porpoises, we need to learn much more about their movements and habitat needs. Then there must be public pressure to convince governments to establish reserves. Sometimes, this involves buying the surrounding land from industry or private individuals. It may also require rerouting oil tankers and other ship traffic. Only if we reserve safe homes for dolphins and porpoises and then protect them can we count on the wonder of their company in the future.

The habitat needs of dolphins and porpoises are becoming better known as researchers study species in their natural surroundings. Orcas off Vancouver Island use shallow beaches along the coast as rubbing areas. An orca, *far left*, swims on its back as it waits its turn to rub on the smooth underwater pebbles. This marine region and an adjacent land area called the Robson Bight/ Michael Bigg Ecological Reserve have been set aside as a protected site for orcas. More than 150 orcas use the reserve almost every day, especially during the summer months. Besides rubbing, they play, rest and sometimes feed on salmon. Despite this protection, orca pods face an uncertain future. Intensive logging, *left*, continues in the area. In the past, logging near river valleys and log booms in estuaries have destroyed salmon runs. Both salmon fishermen and orcas depend on healthy salmon populations. In addition, increased shipping activity and road building bring more human traffic as well as water pollution from streams to rivers to estuaries. No one knows how much change orcas and other dolphins and porpoises can tolerate in their habitat. But prudence dictates a cautious approach, unless we want dolphins and porpoises to disappear forever from our shores.

The Bottlenose Dolphin
S. Leatherwood and R.R. Reeves
(editors)
Academic Press; San Diego; 1990

*Dolphin Societies: Discoveries
and Puzzles*
K. Pryor and K.S. Norris (editors)
University of California Press;
Berkeley and Oxford; 1991

*Dolphins, Porpoises and Whales of the
World. The IUCN Red Data Book*
M. Klinowska
IUCN; Gland, Switzerland, and
Cambridge, UK; 1991

*A Field Guide to the Whales,
Porpoises and Seals of the Gulf of
Maine and Eastern Canada: Cape
Cod to Newfoundland*
S.K. Katona, V. Rough and
D.T. Richardson
Scribner's; New York; 1983

The Greenpeace Book of Dolphins
J. May (editor)
Sterling; New York; 1990

Lads Before the Wind
K. Pryor
Harper & Row; New York; 1975

*Meeting the Whales: The Equinox
Guide to Giants of the Deep*
E. Hoyt
Camden House Publishing;
Camden East, Ontario; 1991

*The Natural History of Whales &
Dolphins*
P.G.H. Evans
Facts on File; New York; 1987

Orca: The Whale Called Killer
E. Hoyt
Camden House Publishing;
Camden East, Ontario; 1990

*The Sierra Club Handbook of Whales
and Dolphins*
S. Leatherwood, R.R. Reeves and
L. Foster
Sierra Club Books; San Francisco;
1983

Whales, Dolphins and Porpoises
R. Harrison and M.M. Bryden
(editors)
Merehurst; London; 1988

*The World of the Bottlenosed
Dolphin*
D.K. Caldwell and M.C. Caldwell
J.B. Lippincott; Philadelphia; 1972

Two popular magazines devoted to
dolphins and porpoises, as well as
whales, are *Whalewatcher*, available from the American Cetacean
Society, Box 4416, San Pedro,
California 90731; and *Sonar*,
available from the Whale and
Dolphin Conservation Society,
19A James Street W., Bath, Avon,
England BA1 2BT.

Conversion Chart		
To Change	Into	Multiply by
centimetres	inches	0.4 (0.394)
metres	feet	3 (3.28)
kilometres	miles	0.6 (0.62)
sq. kilometres	sq. miles	0.4 (0.386)
kilograms	pounds	2.2 (2.205)
Celsius	Fahrenheit	1.8 and add 32

INDEX